ENOUGH ALREADY

ENOUGH ALREADY

From the struggle
to be enough...
To the realization I am
Enough Already.

LINDSEY WEIGLE

Enough Already

By Lindsey Weigle

Copyright © 2021 by Lindsey Weigle

Cover © 2021 by Lindsey Weigle

Primary Editor: Kim Foster – www.kimfostereditor.com

Cover and Interior Design: Rene Folsom & Stacey Smekofske – www. editsbystacey.com

Published by LW Publishing

For further information about speaking engagements, professional consultation, special bulk pricing, or other related inquiries, see the author's website. www.lindseyweigel.com

To learn more about the DreamSMALL program—our online, self-paced behavior change program—email benslow@bluewateradvisory.com.

To learn more about the coaching and training at Bluewater Advisory, visit www.bluewateradvisory.com.

ISBN Print: 978-1-7367079-0-6

Digital: 978-1-7367079-1-3

First Printing

To my parents for giving me the tools to find my way to enough-ness.

To my husband for always seeing my enough-ness,
even when I couldn't.

To my kids for whom I hope my journey to
enough-ness makes yours a little easier.

CONTENTS

Am I creating the life I want or managing the life I've got?

— LINDSEY WEIGLE

INTRODUCTION

I have read a lot of "this kind of book" in my day. I have always been attracted to the stories of others and the paths they've walked and the insights they've gained. Some books are captivating, leaving me disappointed they are over but inspired to go out and live a better life. Some are too hard to get through, dripping with preachy-ness and an eye-rolling amount of self-absorption. Mostly, however, these books always help me think about one or two things in my life that I can make better. They leave me with something I can take away and implement to make my life different than it was before I read it.

The ones I connect with and value (and recommend) the most are the ones that are real, relatable, and share some truth I already feel in my soul. They put words on paper that make me realize some truth about myself that I didn't know anyone else experienced. They make me feel less alone and my days a little better. This is my hope for you.

By sharing my truths and lessons, I hope you connect with them in a way that makes your life a little better. That you hear a truth that you also recognize in your life or that you are relieved to hear someone else felt or experienced. Although my story is unique to my situation, I know for a fact it is not a unique experience.

My journey didn't start out as a journey. It started out a day like any other. But it was one that led me to discover real truths about myself and the way I was living my life. In the next hundred or so pages, you will hear how numerous encounters with books, podcasts, movies, thought leaders, and personal friends helped to reshape the way I interacted with the world and within myself. By paying attention to these interactions, I crafted a healthier and more sustainable life. There was no list of "ten things" or "three steps" to be happier on my journey. There were only insights and ahas gained day by day through these seemingly innocuous places and then putting the work in to choose the behaviors and life I wanted to lead.

On the other side, I could not be more grateful to share my story with you in hopes that my experience, lessons learned from others, and the work I put in have some positive impact on your days as well. More than anything, however, I hope you realize that you, too, are enough. Just as you are. In every flaw, every wrinkle, every imperfection, and every bit of magic.

You. Are. Enough.

I'M FINE. I AM TOTALLY FINE

"You seem stressed."

My doctor's words hit me hard.

"Actually, up until a month ago, I had never felt better. I was working out nearly every day, eating better than ever, making time for myself." I replied to her statement with a matter-of-factness that struck even me as trying too hard.

My energy had been off lately. About a month earlier, I felt like I was coming down with the flu but never actually got sick. And the exhaustion just wouldn't go away. No matter how much sleep I got, I woke up every morning exhausted and had to work extra hard just trying to get to the end of the day. I was hoping to get some blood work done to right whatever was wrong. I assumed it was an easy fix, a B_{12} issue like I had in high school. Or maybe it was my thyroid. My mom had a thyroid issue, so I figured it was probably something like that. I was sure I just needed a pill or a vitamin, and I would be back to normal in no time.

The doctor agreed to the blood work I requested, and I happily walked to the lab to get all the answers I needed. That blood work, as it turned out, was the beginning of the end—and the beginning of it all.

"I need you to take me to brunch."

The text went out on Saturday afternoon to my Wolfpack, a group of four friends with eight kids between us. You know those friends. The group with various parenting styles, different personalities, different lifestyles, different hair color and laughs. Yet all of us so similar too, similar in heart, similar in thoughtfulness, and similar in deep love and support for each other. These are the women who always have my back, who go out of their way to support me, encourage me, and make me feel human. The women who love my kids as their own. The women who get me. We were fortunate that fate put us together a few years earlier, and we instantly recognized how lucky we were to have found each other.

It was the day after my blood work came back. All the test results were normal. I was perfectly healthy. I was shocked. It didn't make any sense. How could I be perfectly fine? What had me feeling so rundown? How was I going to fix this if I didn't know what was causing it? What concerned me even more, however, was what I saw in my healthcare app. I discovered that every April for the past three years, I had gone to the doctor and asked for the same blood work to be done because I had the same mysterious symptoms.

How had I not realized that? And why did I have these same symptoms every year with no answers as to the cause? I was both concerned and annoyed at the same time. I needed friends to commiserate with, to bitch to, to drink mimosas with, to escape real life for a few hours with, and to recharge my batteries with. I thought brunch was the answer to all my worries, but in reality, I should have known that brunch wasn't going to fix this.

Looking back now, it seems so clear that the problem wasn't related to my physical health, that what was going on wasn't something easily fixable with a vitamin or daily pill. That instead, it was something bigger, something that would require soul searching and growth. Something that would become undeniable and unavoidable all too soon and require me to confront the hard truths about myself. But of course, I didn't know any of that just yet. I still thought mimosas with my Wolfpack was the answer to all my problems.

"We are worried about you. You know that we love you and think the world of you, but you have too much on your plate. You run yourself too hard." My Wolfpack sat across the table from me with concern in their eyes and love in their words.

"We have no idea how you do all that you do. Your lifestyle isn't sustainable. You have to cut yourself some slack, and you have to find a way to share the workload. You are going to burn yourself out."

I adored their concern and perhaps even felt a little validated in learning that they saw how hard I ran and how much I did. But instead of truly listening to them and processing what they were saying, their words slid off me like suntan lotion on wet skin.

Sure, I ran hard, but didn't everyone? And it's not like I *wanted* to run that hard, I *had* to run that hard. I had two young kids, was a partner in a growing consulting business and did the majority of kid and home care because my husband was gone twelve hours a day for work. What else was I *supposed* to do? I got up every day, did what needed to be done, had a glass of wine at night, and flung myself into bed. Isn't that what everyone did?

Why were my friends so worried about me? I was fine. Totally fine. I worked hard to deflect their concerns. I told them I knew how it looked, and while certainly there were times I had a lot on my plate, with kids this young and a career I loved so much, busy was to be expected. I assured them that with friends like them and mimosa brunches more often, I would be just fine. I could tell they didn't believe me and wanted to discuss this further, but they also knew how incredibly stubborn I was and that it was likely I wouldn't listen anyway. They told me they loved me and they were there for me.

I smiled and reassured them. "I'm fine. I am totally fine. I promise." We finished our mimosas, took a picture to commemorate another fabulous Wolfpack get-together, and all headed home.

That afternoon found me consumed with all the "doing" that is required with two little kids and very busy days. But even in the busyness, I just couldn't shake what I had heard from my friends that morning.

Prepping dinner. "You have too much on your plate."

Picking up the living room. "Your lifestyle isn't sustainable."

Washing the dishes. "We are worried about you."

Answering work emails. "You run yourself too hard."

Folding laundry. "You have to cut yourself some slack."

Putting the kids to bed. "The rate at which you are running is too high. You are going to crash."

Their words cycled through my head like the chorus to a song you wish you could get rid of. But by the next morning, I had shaken it off and assured myself they were wrong. I was fine. I just needed an afternoon manicure for some self-care to recharge my batteries and everything would be fine.

Until the moment it happened, I never saw it coming. It was so far off my radar of possibilities that I didn't even know it *could* happen. But it did. The moment that life would abruptly and painfully show me just how far past capacity I had been living. The moment that life would insist I face the consequences and realities on the other side.

THE ENOUGH-NESS VOID

Perky, friendly, hard-working, bossy, energetic. These have always been words used to describe me. They have been my lane, my go-to, the things you loved or hated about me (and sometimes both at the same time), the value I took pride in adding to the world. However, a characteristic you would not find on that list was feeling "enough" in my own skin. I was not gifted a soul that innately owns her own presence, who knows her value, and who feels the cadence of her own pace.

No, I never related to those people who seem to feel so effortlessly comfortable in their own skin. Those who seem to have a vision of how they want to live their lives and clear boundaries as to how they want to be treated by others. There's an ease to the way they live their lives and how they carry themselves. That's never been me. No, instead I was gifted a soul that has always overthought every decision, questioned every move, weighed the pros and cons until the two lists blurred together and left me squarely in inaction.

I've always needed praise and craved feedback in order to feel accomplished. I've strived for acceptance and the approval of others even in the most mundane situations. And most unfortunately, I've always relied on others to fill my "enough-ness" void.

You know that void. It's the place that deeply cares what others think of you, that relies on others' reactions to your actions as a metric to determine whether you did the right thing. The place that constantly compares yourself to others in order to decide where you fall on the spectrum of cool, pretty, happy, organized, funny, captivating, smart, or pretty much anything you hope to be true about yourself. The place that gets defensive when others have a different opinion. The place that feels immense satisfaction when someone praises you, only to realize later how temporary that satisfaction was. The place that is always seeking external validation to create temporary relief from the void that is really there.

This is the place I have spent most of my life operating from and working desperately hard to fill. It's also a void I didn't know I had. It's a place that ruled most of my decision making, relationships, happiness, and certainly my worth and self esteem without me even knowing it. A black hole that existed in my periphery.

LIFE IS A STUBBORN TEACHER

This enough-ness void is the reality that life would force me to confront. This is the lesson life had been trying to teach me over and over again, but I had continually avoided. It was the lesson that life needed me to learn, but I had always found a way around it. In the next few weeks, I would be forced to confront this lesson. Life would make me face my insecurities, my cop-outs, the bruises and the scars I had been operating with for nearly my entire life.

Life has a funny way of doing that. Giving us opportunities to first learn lessons in small, low-consequence situations. Yet so often we choose to look away from the lesson. We walk around the thing that life is trying to make us confront because we don't want to deal with it or because we aren't yet ready to learn what life is trying to teach us.

The truth is, however, that life is a stubborn teacher, and when we decide to ignore the easy lesson, life gets a little louder with the message. The situation is usually different, but the lesson is the same. Only this time the stakes are a little higher and the consequences hit harder than they did the first time around. But do we listen? Usually not. Usually we get through the situation, thankful to have escaped relatively unscathed and return to life as usual. But life does not go gently into that good night. No, life doubles down. The message is sent again. The situation is likely different than before, but the lesson remains the same. Only now the lesson in front of us is bigger, louder, angrier, and harder to ignore. Still somehow, we find a way to skate around truly learning it. We deal with the consequences, lick our wounds, and vow to do better, convinced we will learn from our past mistakes. Yet a few weeks or months later, we inevitably find ourselves walking the same path. That is, until life has had enough.

Life has been the gentle and kind parent; it has been the frustrated teacher and even the loud, scary dictator. And we still choose to walk around the lesson it is so desperate to teach us. Life has no choice but to get down and dirty. It sits dormant for a time, quiet, gathering up all its strength. Then it hits hard and loud and always where you are the most vulnerable.

THE DOING BADGE

I had always been a person who functioned by doing, completing, and succeeding. I was driven by accomplishment and order. I measured the success of my days by how much I had gotten done, like there was a "Doing Badge" waiting for me at the end of the day. Then I had a baby.

Needless to say, that life-altering reality was an aggressive adjustment. With a new baby, there wasn't a whole lot of doing anything but pumping, crying (often both of us), laundry, and exhaustion. I kept telling myself it would get better, that eventually things would get back to normal. I kept hoping, praying, and digging for something to grab onto in order to feel whole, connected, and okay. The harsh reality was that even as time went on, all I felt was loneliness, emptiness, and so . . . much . . . exhaustion.

Here is where I am supposed to say that while the first year as a mom was hard and overwhelming, it was also wonderful and magical. But the truth is, for me, only the first two of those adjectives were true. I loved my daughter, I really did (and do, more than anything), but that didn't change the reality that I struggled to connect with anything in motherhood but the hard, the tired, the alone, and the sad. I was a person who found worthiness through achieving, organizing, and accomplishing. That first year of motherhood I felt deprived of all those things. I remember so desperately wanting to find something that made me feel accomplished and good enough: a house that was clean enough, a diaper bag that was organized enough, a body that felt fit enough, a conversation that felt engaged enough. Anything—just anything—that was enough instead of the inadequate, deflated, fat, tired, disorganized mess that I felt at every single turn in my life.

On top of it all, the deep exhaustion I experienced after a long day of work and newborn-momming was all-encompassing and relentless. It was nearly impossible to do anything but the bare minimum of keeping her content and our household surviving. One particular day, I had enough of the chaos and decided it was time to do something about it. I put her to bed and headed downstairs, determined to get a sense of normalcy back in our house and a sense of accomplishment out of my day no matter how long it took. I had nothing left in my tank but found a final gear in the day to pick up the house, do a few loads of laundry, wash the dishes and bottles, clean up the toys, and vacuum.

As I folded the last onesie and put it in the basket to take upstairs with me, I sighed a deep sigh in both exhaustion and pride in what I had accomplished that night. As I dragged myself up the stairs to bed, laundry basket on my hip, I stopped and looked down at the living room. I had drained my tank, given it all I had, and found a way to accomplish cleaning the house. As I continued my climb, I stopped and laughed. I realized that while I was incredibly proud of myself for cleaning the house, in reality, the house was not something "pre-baby" Lindsey would ever have considered as clean or worthy of pride.

As I ascended the next step, I thought about that difference and felt a rush of sadness envelope me. It was the realization of how different my life was and that even when I worked past my maximum capacity, it was likely that nothing I ever did would feel good enough again. My best was wimpy, a cop-out, a failure. No matter how hard I tried, I would never find a way to truly be good enough. By the last step, my brain was fried, and my heart was heavy as I went to bed.

THE "GOOD MOM" TEST TUBE

A few days after the soul-crushing house cleaning experience, I was on the phone with my girlfriend, Courtney. She's the one I can tell anything to, the one who knows my dark and twisty side and loves me even more for it. She could hear how stressed and completely overwhelmed I was at that time. She was pushing me to cut myself some slack, to recognize all I had on my plate, and to find a way to lighten the load, but I wasn't ready to hear it yet.

During my protest that there was "no way to do less," that this was "just my life now and I needed to find a way to suck it up and be better at all of it," it's like a light bulb went off. In that moment, I could clearly see that my life was divided into sections. As a visual, I think of them as a rack of test tubes. Every test tube had at least one hundred lines to reach in order to be filled. There was a test tube for a clean house, a bed made every morning, perfectly organized closets, a spotless fridge, dusted furniture, clean countertops and baseboards, vacuumed floors, spotless bathrooms, etc. There was also a test tube for my profession, a tube for organization, a tube for socialization, a tube for giving to others. The list of tubes went on and on.

These were the terms of measurement I used to judge myself daily. I lived my days trying to fill each of these test tubes to the brim. During my conversation with Courtney, I realized that being a mom had added another test tube—a complex, enormous, draining test tube that I was working desperately hard to fill while still trying to fill all the other tubes.

This "Good Mom" test tube included another one hundred things: creating a structured day for my daughter, introducing foods at the right time, getting her on a sleep schedule, having stockpiled diapers, reading to her, knowing if she should have a pacifier or not, pumping (…oh the pumping), playing with her, having clean and washed bottles when I needed them, and doing it all gracefully and lovingly, even as she screamed her face off at me for the fourth hour in a row with little to no sleep under my belt.

Somehow, I had added this giant tube with a thousand lines to hit but still expected to be able to fill all my old tubes to the same level as I did before. It had never occurred to me that perhaps that wasn't realistic, that I was indeed asking way more out of myself than any human could be expected to accomplish. Before that conversation, I genuinely believed the bare minimum was achieving 100% perfection in every category and doing it with a smile.

During our conversation I came to the sobering realization that perhaps it wasn't feasible. The only way to remain functional was to recognize I had to lower my standards and accept that perfection in every aspect of life isn't achievable or healthy. I began to explore the idea that perhaps achieving 80% in each of these tubes would have to be my new 100%. I hoped this realization and adjustment of expectation would lead me to feeling accomplished, whole, and enough.

Unfortunately, this was a lesson I chose to walk around. Instead of pausing to look more deeply at what was going on, I avoided the struggles I was facing and missed the opportunities to figure out why I was so hell-bent on running myself ragged. Over the next few years, life would give me multiple opportunities to learn this lesson, to help me recognize the enough-ness void that was silently running my life. We would add another baby to the family, only further rooting my behavior in working myself to the bone. There would be meltdowns and screaming fits and overwhelming frustrations, yet I would continue to sidestep the real issue going on. Instead, I chose to deal with the trouble in front of me, resolved to do better and carried on living the way I had always been living.

But true to form, life would gain speed. Life would increase the consequences of a lesson not learned until it would strike so boldly that I could no longer walk around it. Life was determined to show me my enough-ness void and all those obstacles I had in my way.

Enough-ness note: I can now see that I used these test tubes in an attempt to achieve enough-ness. I believed that if I could be clean *enough*, organized *enough*, hardworking *enough*, I could fill my void and finally find enough-ness. But as I now know, enough-ness doesn't come from achieving. It would take me months of soul-searching and hard work to discover the deeper truth around how my behaviors and beliefs were rooted in my lack of enough-ness. but that doesn't make the realization I had on this particular day any less meaningful. It was true. I did expect too much out of myself, I did have my standards set far too high. But this was only the first layer I had to peel back to discover the ultimate truth—that I already was enough.

THE MOMENT

It was a morning like any other morning. I woke up to a kid yelling into a baby monitor, "Mommy, I need to use the pee!" That's the adorable way my youngest announced he had to go to the bathroom. I took a deep breath, rolled out of bed, headed to get him and begin the day. It was Sunday, which meant I made homemade pancakes, a favorite ritual of mine that included making them in fun shapes to reduce breakfast-eating negotiation, while also allowing me to make a double batch to get us through breakfasts during the rest of the week.

As I wrapped up cleaning the kitchen, I was thinking about what needed to be done next when out of nowhere, an overwhelming numbness hit me. I stood there for a minute staring at the counter. I felt everything and nothing all at once. It was like a tidal wave of feathers; incredibly intense but also so light. I just stood there staring into space for what seemed like an eternity.

Just standing there.

Eventually, I grew tired of standing, but I didn't have the energy to go anywhere. I slid down the cabinets and plopped onto the floor; the pressure from the cabinets on my back so comforting. Then I just sat there, unable to do or think about anything. I have no idea how long I sat on the kitchen floor, staring into nothingness, but it was the only thing I could bring myself to do. My husband came into the kitchen and looked down at me confused and asked if I was okay. I looked at him and said, "Actually, I don't think so." He looked at me, still confused but now slightly concerned. After a long pause, I looked up at him and said, "I think I need a minute."

Up until that moment, I am not sure I had ever admitted to myself, let alone anyone else, that I wasn't okay. I was always the person who, when the water started rising, built a bigger boat. The one who dug a little deeper, who found a way to make it happen and to be okay while doing it. Sure, I complained to my parents and my girlfriends about being stressed and being crazy busy, but I had so tightly shoved "okay-ness" into my soul that it would never have occurred to me to consider if I was truly okay or not. I simply *had* to be okay.

But in this moment, there was no deeper to dig. There was no bigger boat to build. In that moment, there wasn't even a boat. I stood up, walked to the bathroom, and collapsed on the floor, crying more tears than I would have believed was humanly possible. I spent an hour sobbing on the floor without entirely knowing what was causing the tears or how to make them stop. Eventually I dragged myself from the bathroom to my bed where I spent the rest of the day unable to do much of anything except oscillate between staring at the wall and sobbing. It's as though I had a lifetime of tears to cry out, and now that I had started, there just was no stopping them.

My natural tendency when stressed or overwhelmed was always to barrel through, but for the first time ever, instead of fighting, I gave in and let the riptide take me. Somewhere through all the tears, the bubbles of a life lived too hard began to surface. I began to feel how much I had on my plate, to acknowledge the stress my lifestyle was causing me, to feel the mom guilt that was eating me alive, to look realistically at the outrageously high expectation I held myself to, to accept that I could not carry the load I had put on myself any longer, to allow myself to hit the pause button on the breakneck speed of my life, and to sink deeply into the reality of the unsustainable life I had been living.

My husband checked in on me every twenty minutes or so, asking if I was okay and what he could do. The answers were always the same: "I don't know" and "nothing." My dam of stress, frustration, overwhelm, and exhaustion had just broken free and there was nothing I could do to stop it.

I laid in my bed for the rest of the afternoon and into the evening. The tears that I thought would never end eventually began to subside. But in their place, a numbness was left. The weight of the realizations that had forced their way to the surface and the shock of finally feeling all of them melded together left me in a nearly catatonic daze. Somewhere along the way, I fell into a deep sleep, resigned to see where the morning would find me.

I woke up the next morning still in a daze but more functional than the day before. Though it was a bit like living underwater. I felt like I was in slow motion. Everything took so much more effort than normal. The following days found me alternating between mostly functional and an uncontrollable sobbing mess. But no matter what state I was in, I couldn't shake the numbness. It was like living in an alternate reality where I had no control over my body. I was simply an observer of my life, watching it take place with no say in what was happening.

It was tempting to want to will my way out of the crying and the numbness. To revert to my old habits of "sticking it in my toes" and forcing myself to be okay. I mean, I certainly didn't want my kids to see me living in a state of sporadic involuntary sobbing, and it didn't seem fair to my husband to have to carry so much of the household load as I fell apart. But I knew at a deep level that pretending to be okay wasn't the right answer. It probably wasn't even possible. The dam had broken and there was no way to convince myself I was okay any longer. It was time to face the tide.

I spent a lot of time thinking back over the past few years of the struggles I had experienced, the roadblocks I had hit, and the meltdowns that had blindsided me (there was a doozy that started with a messy art closet and ended with me crying at the bar in a Buffalo Wild Wings on a Saturday afternoon, but that story is for another book). I started to realize this was not the first time I had been asked to confront the reality of my situation. In fact, life had been trying to teach me this lesson for years. I could see that life had smacked me in the face with this lesson more than a few times, but each time I had ignored, walked around, and avoided the lesson. It was becoming clear that life's attempted lesson had been building steam over the past few years, and it was finally time to unleash the lesson in a way I could no longer avoid.

Thankfully, however, I knew life's MO. I could see that life had grown tired of trying to teach me this lesson, and if I continued to walk around it, the next time the consequences would be dire. The time for pretending to be okay was over. I was determined to get it right this time, which meant I couldn't just suck it up and go back to business as usual. I had to walk the path of this lesson and face the realities about myself I had been avoiding for so long.

THE AFTERMATH

Three days after my total collapse as a human, I was scheduled to speak in front of a hundred CEOs about a program I had designed to help individuals create the behavior change and goal achievement they wanted in their lives. At first, I wasn't sure I should do it. Frankly, I wasn't even sure I *could* do it. I had begun to notice how much guilt I had been carrying around with me on a daily basis and how much guilt stopped me from doing the things I wanted to do. And even worse, I realized how much joy guilt was stealing from my life.

I had been ecstatic about the opportunity to share my program with the world before my meltdown, but now I worried about leaving my family after I had been in such a rough state. I worried I hadn't "earned" going on this work trip or that I was somehow wrong for being excited to share my program. I could feel the guilt taking hold, but this time I was bound and determined to live in the emotion of excitement instead of guilt and fear, as I was now beginning to realize I had for so many years.

After some soul-searching, it became clear I needed to go. This project was my baby and something I was proud to have created and produced. This was an amazing opportunity to share something that had so profoundly changed my life and that I knew could help others. It was a dream to be able to share my creation with this group of CEOs, and it was opportunity that I didn't want to miss.

I boarded the plane for Atlanta and spent a long day and night preparing, practicing, tweaking, and polishing my presentation. I was grateful for some space to bring this program to life and to share it with the world (well, it felt like the world). I woke up the next morning feeling prepared and ready to take on my presentation. What was shocking, however, was the lack of guilt I felt, which normally accompanied all my work trips. Even when I was working, there was always a gnawing feeling that I was letting my family down, that I wasn't there for those who needed me, that I was disappointing everyone. But this morning the guilt wasn't there. In its place was the clarity that I was there for a reason. I was there to share what I had learned with those who could benefit. I had a job to do and I was proud to do it. My kids were cared for and loved in school and at home with their dad.

In that moment, I felt peace. It was one of the first times since I had become a mom that I remembered feeling contented about a decision I had made. I looked at myself in the mirror, proud I had gotten on the plane, and headed off to the ballroom to kick some ass.

After I boarded the plane home, I sat thinking about how intense the past two weeks had been. I was thrilled with how the CEO session went. I was so grateful I had actually pulled it off and how well it had been received by the group. At a deeper level, I was also thankful for the space to focus on myself for a few days. Not only had I been able to present to the group, but I also saw a tiny glimpse of clarity and focus that I hadn't felt in a very long time.

It had not been an easy decision to go at first, but it became clear I had made the right one. I knew I had a long road ahead of me, but I was grateful to have made progress in the right direction. As the wheels left the ground, I closed my eyes and began to figure out how I was going to put the pieces of my life back together. This time, in a way that worked for my mental and physical health.

BURNOUT

Upon returning home, I quickly made an appointment with a therapist. I had gone to therapy a decade earlier and it was wonderfully helpful in getting me through a rough patch in my life (thanks to an amazing therapist). I was hopeful this experience would be equally as wonderful. I sat in the waiting room with every last bit of hope that the answer to my struggles would be on the other side of the door, just as I had at the doctor's office.

The therapist called my name. I calmly walked into her office, trying to be oh-so-put-together, and sat in the chair. She smiled sweetly at me and looked at the pre-session paperwork I had filled out in the lobby.

"What brings you in today?"

I smiled and began to explain what could only be described as the nervous breakdown I had experienced two weeks earlier and what had gotten me there. I matter-of- factly ran through the list of things I had on my plate, explained the guilt I felt at every turn, and the ridiculous level of expectation I held myself to as quickly as I could so as to not bore her with all the "test tubes" of my life. (Feeling as though you are bothering your therapist should be a pretty clear indication that you have a lot to work through.)

She looked at me with sympathetic eyes and said, "Oh, my. It's no wonder you had that attack. Anyone with that much on their plate would suffer from burnout. I am just surprised you didn't burn out sooner."

I sat quietly and began to absorb her words.

Burnout. *Hmmm.*

Burnout? *Really?*

Burnout? *That's all that was?*

Burnout. *Isn't that an excuse for wimpy people?*

Burnout . . .

Oh my gosh.

Yes. *Burnout.*

Damn. Burnout is REAL.

Burnout is unforgiving.

I. Have. Burnout.

It took me more than a minute to process the diagnosis of burnout. Then tears…so many tears. There were those floodgates again. I cried and cried and cried as I tried to process. I had crashed. I had burned. I had burned *out*. Until that day, it had never occurred to me that I could hit a point I couldn't recover from, a limit I could hit. I had always assumed if I just worked hard enough, gritted my teeth and pushed forward enough, everything would be fine. I prided myself on being able to handle more than other people, believing I was tougher than most and most assuredly superhuman.

Burnout. That single word shattered the pillar on which I had built my identity. The rock upon which I had built my being, the "can-doer" I had always been. To face the reality that I was not superhuman as I had previously believed was both shocking and liberating. It ignited the realization that I was, in fact, a mere mortal who had been unnecessarily carrying the weight of the world around on her shoulders, and it was time to take off the cape. It had never occurred to me there might be a mountain too high, a plate too full, a lifestyle too aggressive, a martyrdom too heavy for me to carry. But now, I could see it so clearly, and it was magical.

After I composed myself, she asked me why I carried so much around on my shoulders. Why did I get to the point of burnout? I began to list all the things I had on my plate again, slightly annoyed that she apparently hadn't listened the first time. She stopped me mid-sentence.

"No," she said. "That's *how* you got to burnout. That's easy to see. I asked *why* you got to the point of burnout." I sat quietly again for a minute, processing the difference.

Why *was* I such a doer? Why *did* I place such a high value on working myself to the bone? Why did I believe there was no end to my capacity tank? As I began to look objectively at my behavior, the answer became crystal clear.

"Guilt. Guilt and fear of making a decision I will later regret drives almost every decision and action in my life."

> *Enough-ness note*: The deeper answer to that question becomes clear over the course of my journey in the next few months. I would eventually realize that the real reason in trying to do it all was the lack of enough-ness that I felt. I was trying to prove my worthiness to myself and to others through acts of doing and accomplishing. Of course, at this point in my journey, I wasn't aware of this truth. It was buried too deeply below the layers of struggles and beliefs I held to see it clearly at this point. But identifying the guilt I was most certainly carrying around was one of the first layers I needed to work through in order to get to the core issue I was facing: my enough-ness void.

She sighed.

Oh man, I thought to myself, *I've exasperated my therapist. That can't be good.*

Then she uttered words that changed the way I look at life. "Guilt is the most useless emotion…because the people who shouldn't feel it always do, and the people who should feel it never do. So if you feel it, it means you don't need to. So why not just decide to let go of that?"

Holy shit. (Pardon my French, but that is genuinely the only way to describe how profoundly this statement hit me.) Those words hit my soul hard. I know I've heard words like those before. But this time those words struck a chord. How many times have you been told not to feel guilty?

"Don't feel guilty about taking time for yourself. You're a great mom and wife."

"Don't feel guilty about working so much. It's important for your kids to see a working mom who can contribute to the household income."

"Don't feel guilty for seeing your friends. You will be a better partner when you've made time for fun."

You agree with what they are saying, but you also can't shake the guilt that resonates through your core.

I don't know why I was able to hear the truth in that statement on that particular day. Maybe it was because of her bluntness. Maybe it was the fragile state I was in that allowed the message to sneak through my normally impenetrable armor. Maybe I was finally tired of carrying around all that guilt and was so grateful to hear someone tell me it was okay to put it down. For whatever reason, sitting in that therapist's office on that day, it became my mission to let go of the hundreds of pounds of guilt I had been carrying around nearly every day my entire life.

THE UNRAVELING

After leaving the therapist's office that day, I had gotten exactly what I had come for without even knowing it. I was validated by an outside source, someone who had no reason to tell me anything but the absolute truth. I had worked hard enough, I had done enough, I had given up enough. In fact, I had worked too hard, done too much, and given up too much. Somehow, her acknowledgment that I should have burned out sooner cut through all the layers of misguided beliefs I had been wrapping myself in for years. From that day on, my mission became to look more objectively at my life. I needed to figure out what was working for me and to change what wasn't. I became a Lindsey sociologist of sorts, working to observe my life instead of plowing my way through it. I had spent so much of the past five years with my head down, getting from morning to night, weekday to weekend, and vacation to vacation, that I never really stopped to look at the life I was living. I was so busy trying to do it all, I never stopped to decide if it was the life I wanted to live. I was too busy damn near killing myself attempting to make everyone happy that I never stopped to consider if I was happy.

> *Enough-ness note:* The look at my life wasn't about my kids, my husband, or my job, it was about me. It was about taking the time to understand myself. To look at the way I lived my life, the things I believed about myself, and the "must dos" and "must nots" I had played over and over in my head without questioning whether they were healthy, whether they were serving me, or whether they were even true.

I wanted to move from the stress, guilt, and the feeling of never being enough to instead creating the contentedness, peace, happiness, and enough-ness that I wanted in my life. My plan was to stop, to observe, to consider, and to choose action instead of continuing to live in reaction and default behaviors. I needed to reset my behaviors and beliefs in a way that made me happy and, as it turns out, that would ultimately end up making me a better mom, partner, daughter, friend, and human.

I DO. I HAVE. I AM. ENOUGH

Looking back on my life, it's so easy to see all the ways that I tried to feel enough.

> *Maybe I'll be enough if I donate to the less fortunate.*

> *Maybe I'll be enough if I am known as a thoughtful person.*

Maybe I'll feel peace if my house is clean and organized enough.

Maybe I'll feel good enough about myself if I lose the baby weight, my skin is clear enough, my tummy is flat enough, my teeth are white enough.

Maybe I'll feel worthy enough if I vacuum out my car, get all the laundry done, purge the excess clothes from our closets.

Maybe I'll feel secure enough if we have more money in savings, less credit card debt, or have a big enough paycheck.

Enough-ness note: I have come to realize that not everyone is an accomplishment junkie like I am. There are any number of ways that we attempt to fill enough-ness voids. The value is in discovering if you have an enough-ness void and if so, how you try and fill it.

The problem is enough-ness is tricky. Or at least it was for me. Because the void was so big and I didn't know how to fill it, or that I even needed to fill it, I came up with all sorts of ways to temporarily rent it. I would fill the void for small moments of time, convincing myself I could work my way into enough-ness. When the house was cleaned, organized, and purged, I added a little enough-ness into the void. The surge of happiness in seeing the cleanliness and the pride of having worked hard was enough to temporarily glaze over the true lack of enough-ness I felt. But true to a void, it never successfully filled it. It simply relieved the uncomfortableness for a few minutes until the ache of the void returned. Even worse was when the house wasn't cleaned, the car wasn't vacuumed, or dinner wasn't made, the Band-Aid of temporary success was removed. The lack of enough-ness became suffocating.

I did everything for everyone, working so hard but never feeling like it was enough, needing their acknowledgment and thank-you to fill my enough-ness void. And when the thank-you didn't come or it wasn't big enough, I got angry and resentful. Leaving me working harder, doing more, and exhausting myself more deeply in an attempt to receive the praise I so desperately needed.

Potentially even worse, however, was when the thank-you did come, when it was big enough and when I felt seen and appreciated, it filled my enough-ness void, at least temporarily. Renewing my belief that if I worked hard enough, gave up enough, cleaned enough, I could finally feel enough. But because no one person or thing can make you feel enough, I was instead left constantly chasing the unfindable enough-ness.

What I now know is that you don't earn enough-ness. You earn a paycheck. You earn a promotion. You earn a clean kitchen. You earn being seen as a loyal and trustworthy friend. You earn climbing Mount Kilimanjaro. You earn a flat stomach. But none of those things can give you enough-ness.

You can't earn enough-ness because you already are enough in just being you.

SIX TO EIGHT HOURS

Vertical farming. Have you heard of it? It's a pretty amazing process that many companies and individuals are using to grow food with less space and water than traditional farming—and all without pesticides. One day in a meeting, my client mentioned that his company was investing in vertical farms. I had never heard of it. He described it as rows of giant warehouses where plants are stacked vertically in massive columns. Machines are used to administer water and light as necessary to individual plants and crops. As he explained the process, the science, and the possibilities, I was completely intrigued by the concept.

Over the course of the next few weeks, I began reading articles and listening to podcasts about the industry and the mechanics behind it. Part of the draw of this type of farming is the ability to intentionally control the growth of plants and crops and to reduce or eliminate the typically uncontrollable problems. In vertical farming, droughts or overly rainy seasons have no effect on crop production because they are in a controlled environment. There are no pesticides needed because there are no pests! But one of the biggest advantages is that they can maximize the growth of each individual crop through controlled light and water distribution. There are no cloudy days in vertical farming; there is only the specifically targeted amount of light required to maximize the growth of each plant, producing more plants and crops in shorter periods of time and with less space. (Please note: I am neither pro nor con vertical farming. As with everything in life there is good to be found and there are drawbacks. My interest was in learning about the industry both because I had a client investing in vertical farms and because I found the concept fascinating.)

While driving down the road listening to a podcast, I heard something that shocked me. In vertical farming, they have found that plant and crop growth is maximized when the plants are allowed to rest. In an environment where scientists can take away all natural limitations of growth (such as nighttime), they have found that plants produce *more* when they are allowed to rest in darkness six to eight hours per day. I thought about that for a minute. Plants need rest to grow. I found this truth both curiously and magically profound. Even plants, simple organisms whose only job is to grow from a seed into a plant, need to rest. In perfectly controlled environments, while working diligently to give plants exactly what they need to be productive, scientists, engineers, and farmers, all at some point in the day, simply turn off the lights and let the plants rest. (Okay, technically I am sure there is a robot or timer controlling the lights in the building, but the visual of a group of people turning off the lights in a warehouse to let plants rest is pretty fantastic!) The best thing they can do to maximize growth for their plants is to turn off the lights and give them time to recover from the growth of the day.

This may not strike you as particularly life changing, but it was astonishing to me. Because if even plants need to rest, wouldn't it follow that I too would need to rest? As I listened to the farmer talk about the need for plants to rest, the therapist's words rang through my head, "Burnout." In that moment, it was easy to take a step back and see how asking a plant to grow nonstop would lead to a less-than-optimized organism. To recognize that to be at its best, it would need the same sort of pause that the natural day-and-night cycle had afforded plants for millions of years.

Rest involves more than sleeping. I needed a bigger and more meaningful rest—what I have come to understand as "soul rest." The space to breathe, to process, to let my guard down, to just be enough as I was instead of continually pushing to do more. How long had I been trying to grow without allowing for breathing room? How long had I had my proverbial lights on while expecting constant growth and betterment? When was the last time I had allowed myself the time and space to really rest and recharge?

It was in that moment I truly began to see how I had burned out and how the behaviors and beliefs I had lived with for so long had gotten me to that point. I hadn't rested. In fact, I had actively worked against rest, believing that pushing harder and doing more were the ways to find peace. When all along, the answer had been hard work balanced with rest. It was now obvious that not taking care of myself had been a mistake and moving forward was no longer an option.

Taking care of myself wasn't lazy or selfish or weak. Taking care of myself was nonnegotiable for survival. If a plant could figure that out, so could I. The next question to answer was how.

THE MYTH OF SELF-CARE

Self-care. It's a word we hear all the time these days. We think we know what it looks like: getting our hair done, getting a pedicure, reading a book before bed, having brunch with our girlfriends, taking that ever-elusive nap! We are promised that self-care is the answer to our stressful and busy lives. We are told we need to take time for ourselves in order to survive and thrive in a world that is pulling us in a hundred different directions. We are promised that if we do these activities—get the exercise, go for the walk, have the mimosa—we can continue to fuel the busy lives we lead.

If you would have asked me pre-breakdown, I would have adamantly defended the importance of self-care. I would have said how relaxing the manicures I had every other week were and how magical the Wolfpack get-togethers were. I would have discussed the tap class I took every Tuesday night to reconnect with my childhood and take a break from the stress of a hectic week. I would have cited the joy I got from the dance recital where, yes, each June I stood on stage in a sequined onesie and tapped my heart out with a handful of fifty to seventy-five-year-old women for two and a half minutes.

I was a huge proponent of self-care and talked to all my friends about how important it was they took time for themselves. I would have challenged them to come up with a daily or weekly self-care activity and then followed up with them to make sure they were doing it. I would have sworn self-care could save us all. (Though, even I would have admitted the term is so overused today, it's sometimes hard to take seriously.)

As I began to unpack a lifetime of beliefs, decisions, and habits that had gotten me to this place, I wondered why all that self-care hadn't worked. Wasn't self-care supposed to relieve all my stress and recharge my batteries giving me the energy to tackle another day? Shouldn't those dance classes I was taking have helped me avoid burnout? Why hadn't those hour-long manicures de-stressed me enough to survive my life? If self-care was the answer we were all promised, why hadn't it worked for me?

BUBBLE BATHS AND GAS STATIONS

"You have the expectation that somehow if you just squeeze in a little self-care, all will be well. You treat a bubble bath like a stop at the gas station to refill your tank and end up disappointed when your stress returns shortly after emerging from your bubbles to the reality of responsibilities that didn't magically disappear when the water swirled down the drain."[1]

These words stopped me in my tracks. I was reading *It's About Time: The Art of Choosing the Meaningful over the Urgent* by Valorie

Burton (a book I cannot recommend highly enough) when the thought struck me: I *was* treating self-care like a stop at a gas station.

YES! It seemed so obvious, but this was the piece I was missing. I was engaging in self-care activities, but in those activities, I wasn't actually caring for myself.

Sure, I *got* the manicure, but I was squeezing it in between dropping kids off at school and before my first client appointment of the day. I *was* running off to brunch with my girlfriends but spent the entire time thinking about what a bad mom I was for not being at home with my kids. I *did* force myself to go for a walk at the end of the day, but I spent the whole time thinking about what I should have been taking care of at home instead. I engaged in all those self-care activities because I thought that's what I was supposed to do to de-stress my life. But in reality, I *did* treat self-care like a pit stop at a gas station.

How had I missed this? How did I get self-care so wrong? How had I missed that it isn't an item to be put on a to-do list? It is so much more than that. Self-care is a pause, a relief from the stress of a busy life, a moment to breathe.

No wonder those dance classes weren't saving me from myself. If I were being honest, not only was I treating self- care like an item on a to-do list, but it was often as draining as all the other items. Most weeks I didn't feel excited and engaged as I headed to dance class at 7:00 p.m. on a Tuesday night. More often than not, I was exhausted from a long day and lamented going to dance class. I shoved dinner in my mouth as I rushed to throw on dance clothes and grab my dance bag while feeling guilty the entire time for leaving my kids at bedtime. But I thought, *Self-care is important,* so I dragged myself to dance, while berating myself for not having practiced more during the week. After an hour of being frustrated that I couldn't get my Back-Essence-Spank- Step-Bombershay combination just right, I headed home defeated to throw myself into bed, glad I got through another week of dance class.

My manicures weren't leaving me recharged because as I sat in the chair getting my nails done, I was thinking about the twenty things that needed to be done and the ten things I should have been doing instead.

My walks at night weren't helping because I spent the whole walk listening to the guilt in my head that I should be at home cleaning or organizing something. My self-care activities weren't caring for myself at all. They were checklist items done in the belief that they would fuel me long enough to maintain the hyper speed at which I was living my life. A light bulb went off.

Self-care isn't an activity; it's a belief that you are worthy of taking care of yourself.

In fact, it's the giant responsibility of caring for the body, soul, and mind that guide us around this one life: these precious days, months, and years that we have been given. True and meaningful self-care stems from the belief that we are worthy of both being cared for by others and even more importantly, caring for ourselves. For me, it's been moving self-care away from a task to complete and into making self- care a mindset. That I need and deserve a refresh, a rest, a time-out a few minutes to let go of the weight of the world and just be. Self-care *was* a piece to the puzzle, just not the way I had been doing it.

ENOUGH WITH THE FILTERS

A few months after hitting my burnout point, our family embarked on our annual beach vacation. Every year, we head to the same spot in Nags Head in the Outer Banks of North Carolina. My husband's family has been vacationing there for nearly thirty-five years, and I have joined them for the last decade or so. It's a magical week of relaxation, fun, and family. It had been only a few months since my world had been flipped upside down, and I was trying to soak up every minute of pause and relaxation our vacation had to offer.

The last evening, I sat on the deck of our beautiful beach house and began reflecting on what had been another perfect beach day. I started with early morning yoga on the beach, followed by an entire day spent in the sun and sand with family, including a one-year-old who, after lunch, fell asleep on my lap under a shady umbrella, and with his deep breathing lulling me into a beach nap with him. Finally, an early seafood dinner at our favorite restaurant. As far as days go, it was pretty wonderful. But then again, every day that week had been nearly as flawless. It had been a wonderful vacation.

As the sun set, the sky turned every shade of pink and orange that God ever made. I grabbed my phone and took a picture because it was just so breathtaking. As I shared the beautiful sunset on Facebook, I made sure to add the hashtag #nofilter because I wanted everyone to see how beautiful the sky truly was. In that moment, it occurred to me how much beauty and joy I had seen over the past week. Beautiful sunrises, tiny crabs in the sand, thrilled faces as the ocean waves tossed the kids around at the shore, laughter around the kitchen table during game nights.

There had been so much unfiltered joy and happiness for the entire week. There also had been a lot of moments of imperfection—a bathing suit that hadn't fit as well as it had before I had babies, screaming kids when we dragged them off the beach at the end of each long day, ocean-soaked hair that made me look more like a Russian hockey player than a sun goddess, a nose that apparently had been missed during that last round of sunscreen and left me looking a bit like I had a clown nose in nearly every photo.

I then thought about how often we only see filtered versions of life on social media. Complexion-enhancing apps, taking a dozen photos to get the perfect "post-able" one, avoiding pictures that have us at an unflattering angle, only posting photos that shows us having a great time or the most highlighted moments of our lives. The list of the ways we filter ourselves on social media goes on and on.

I looked at the sunset and thought about the week of pure unfiltered enjoyment I was living. I wondered what it would be like to focus on living free of judgement, free of the desire of creating perfection and instead focus on creating the life I wanted to live. What if I strived to embrace both the wonderful and the imperfect equally? What if I surrounded myself with beauty and things that brought me joy? What if I slowed down enough to notice the magic around me? It occurred to me that a great place to start would be on social media. To stop telling myself and the world that only the perfect is worth posting.

It was in that moment that I vowed never to filter another personal photo on social media. I committed to posting photos that showed the reality of my life and where I was. But even more importantly, I committed to living unfiltered in nearly every aspect of my life, not just on social media. To own my flaws and my strengths. To embrace the hardship and the fun. Not to judge myself against impossible standards.

Enough-ness note: I have allowed touch-ups in photos for marketing in my profession and for this book. Marketing is still a grey area for me that I still need to figure out where I draw the line. But as far as personal and professional, non-marketing social media, I still hold true to this unfiltered commitment to myself.

Enough with the filters. Enough with all the perfection. Enough with all the doing. Enough with the chaos, the stress, the self-loathing, the guilt, and the heartache. I had finally had enough already.

FOUR PIECES OF PIE

As I came to understand self-care through a different set of lenses, the saying "You can't pour from an empty cup" kept floating around my head. It was becoming increasingly obvious that not only had I not been filling my cup, I didn't even have a cup left. All of the times in my life I worked so hard to prove my enough-ness to others, every time I refused to let others help me when I needed it, every time I fought so desperately for the thank-you and recognition, I was slowly chipping away at my own cup.

Every time I weighed the opinions of others over that of my own, every time I let guilt win, every time I chose what was best for someone else over what was mentally healthy for me, I gave away my cup bit by bit. I thought getting validation from others would fill my cup, but instead, those validation-seeking activities were giving it away until there was nothing left. It became very clear that not only did I need to figure out how to start filling my cup, but I needed to figure out how to make one to refill.

For a long time, I believed the unhealthy tapes that played in my head. I believed the societal views of what we are told womanhood and motherhood are all about. I believed in the "do it all, have it all, be it all" as a bare minimum for enough-ness. One day, midway through the overhaul of my mental wellness journey, I was on Facebook. It was the day before Mother's Day, and I was killing some time scrolling. I saw a post that stopped me in my tracks. "A mother is a person who, seeing there are only four pieces of pie for five people, promptly announces she never did care for pie."[2]

A year earlier, I would have internalized that post as a reminder that not only do Good Moms sacrifice what they love for those around them, they also go out of their way to ensure no one sees their suffering. They don't eat the pie they want *and* they ensure everyone thinks they don't even like it. Good Moms never put someone else out. Good Moms sacrifice and they do so quietly and with no expectation of being cared for in return. Good Moms do for others and do without for themselves.

The message here isn't about pie (because frankly, I don't even like pie, so I would happily announce I didn't like it). No, the message here is that the expectation of being a Good Mom is unending sacrifice. As I read the post over and over, I realized I had spent so much of my life giving in to this very notion. I had internalized this belief and had been living this very sentiment. I had worked so hard to be a Good Mom. I had sacrificed quietly, so quietly that no one had noticed. I didn't ask for pie or for help or even for a place at the table, because that's what I told myself Good Moms do. But I now began to see the toll on my soul. The quiet chipping away of my cup and the slow burn toward my burnout.

A few weeks went by and the quote continued to bounce around my head. How long had I been announcing I didn't like pie? And even worse, how many times had I announced I didn't like pie and then got angry when they all ate pie without me? How long had I hoped that after announcing I didn't like pie, someone would see through me and insist I have a piece? How many times had I given up something I really wanted so I could check the Good Mom box, while leaving myself totally depleted? The answer was clearly too many.

Over the next few weeks, I began noticing how often I gave away my pie. It was shocking how many times I made sacrifices that were taxing, exhausting, and totally unnecessary. To see how often I could have asked for the help I needed or even accepted what was offered. It became clear that running myself to the point of exhaustion was my default. I did it without thinking and wore it as a badge of honor. "The more exhausted you are, the closer to enough you must be" seemed to be my unintentional mantra. It was becoming easy to see why I never bothered to fill my own cup and even easier to see how I ended up giving it away without noticing. Who needs a cup when you've already given away your pie?

The "Good Moms announce they don't like pie" message was something I couldn't let go of. One day while driving alone in the car, I got to thinking about the messages we hear about being a Good Mom and how they fit into my life. As I grew more and more angry at the thought of that message, I blurted out, "What kind of crap is that?"

Why should the expectation be that I have to give away everything to ensure other people are happy? What kind of life does that leave for me as a Good Mom? What message does that send to the people in my life about how to treat me? And more importantly, what example does that send to my daughter and son about what Good Moms do?

In that moment, it became clear this was a message I no longer wanted to believe. As a person determined to change unhealthy beliefs, this shot to the top of my list. I realized that just because I had spent a lifetime internalizing this belief didn't mean I had to continue believing it. I needed to find a way to care for others while still caring for myself. I decided it was time to create my own definition of how I was going to be a Good Mom. There had to be a better way than giving up everything in order to care for others. I realized that asking to be included and considered isn't selfish; it's necessary.

It was time to stay at the table and ask for pie. It was time to get creative, to find a way to make another pie or cut the four slices into five. Anything. Anything would be better than continuing to remove myself from the equation entirely. Sustaining an unending tank of self-sacrifice while expecting nothing in return isn't heroism; it's martyr-dom. It's also a pretty great way to lead to total burnout and resentment.

As time has passed, my fury has died down, and I give more grace to the message conveyed in the quote. However, my struggle is when messages like this are the loudest and potentially the only kind we receive about how to be a Good Mom. I get frustrated when an unat-tainable standard of being a Good Mom is set for us. I think, instead, we get to decide how we define ourselves and how we show up as people and as Good Moms. The lesson I took away is about taking a step back to examine what we are buying into and to move past external expectations that are doing more harm than good. I learned to listen more intently to myself and to set my own path that is truer to who I am and how I want to live.

WALK THROUGH THE MUD

I hit a particularly rough patch in my mid-twenties that I ignored until it became undeniably clear I needed help. One particularly hard Thurs-day, I found myself sobbing at my desk at work. Before anyone could find me crying, I closed my office door. While I had been trying to ignore all that was going on in my life (does this sound familiar?), crying at my desk was a pretty clear indicator it was time for some help. I picked up the phone, opened a Google search, looked for a ther-apist close to work, and left voicemails for more than a dozen thera-pists. With quiet resolve to work through the issues in my life, I patiently waited for the therapists to call me back so I could select the right one to work with on my journey.

It turned out, the selection process was easier than I planned, as out of the entire list of therapists I called that afternoon, only one of them called me back. I answered the phone and the kind and cheerful voice on the other end made me instantly feel as though I were in good hands. I have come to believe that life/God/the universe, call it what you will, is always conspiring in our favor. My experiences have shown me that life is smarter than us and is desperately trying to take care of us, if only we will get out of its way and let it. The very foundation of that belief comes from both my experiences during this difficult time and that I connected with Dr. Jill Allen, LMSW, MASSW.

Over the course of a few months, I began to process the situations, people, and feelings that needed figuring out in my life. I also avoided taking any actions on the things that needed action-taking.

One day, Dr. Jill looked at me and said, "Lindsey, we've been doing this for a while now. You are eventually going to have to walk through the mud on this one." I tilted my head to the side like a prairie dog when it comes out of its hole. (That is apparently my go-to move, as almost every photo I have of myself involves this head tilt.)

"I don't know what you mean."

She then gave me some of the wisest advice I have ever received and have passed on to others for more than a decade.

"In life, there are all these mud puddles," she began. "They are the sticky spots, the tough spots, the scary spots in life. Often, because they are so scary, we simply find ways to walk around the mud puddles and avoid getting dirty. The thing about mud puddles, though, is that even when we walk around them, they never really go away. We will continue to face the same mud puddle over and over until we are brave enough to walk through it. You are standing at the edge of your biggest mud puddle. You just have to decide if you are ready to walk through it."

As I processed what she was saying, I formed the most vivid picture in my mind of a mud puddle in front of me. I could see myself standing in a beautiful green meadow with a bright blue sky and soft white rolling clouds behind me. I could feel a slight breeze and the warmth of the sun on my shoulders. I could also see an expansive brown mud puddle only inches from my toes. I had been at this mud puddle before. It was the one I pretended didn't exist. The one I had been bumping into for the last few years. The one I continued to reach the edge of, wondering if I should walk through it but always simply turned around and headed back to the meadow, leaving the mud puddle for another day.

That day, however, was the day I decided it was time to stop avoiding and walk through it. "Let's do it. Let's walk through the mud puddle!" I stated excitedly.

"Great!" she responded. "But here is the thing about mud puddles you need to know. You are going to start walking through this mud puddle, and the mud is going to reach your ankles. You will begin to feel uncomfortable. Then, as you continue to walk, the ground underneath you will slope downward, and the mud will reach your knees, making it hard to walk. The ground will continue to slope downward, and the mud will reach your waist, and then your chest, and it's going to get scary. As you continue, the mud will reach your throat, and you will begin to worry about how deep the mud puddle is. You will take another step, and as the ground continues to slope downward, the mud will come right under your nose. It's in that moment that you will be sure you are going to drown. You will be convinced the mud is too deep to cross, and instinctively you are going to want to turn around to escape the mud.

"But here is the thing you must know to beat the mud. When you take that final step, the one that seems impossible, the one that makes you feel as though you will surely be swallowed whole, that is when the ground under you will begin to slope upward. That final brave step, when the mud is right under your nose, is when you conquer your mud puddle. Surely, there will still be more steps to take, but they get easier and easier. *I promise you, if you walk through the mud you will not drown, but please know it's going to feel as though you will.*"

Over the next weeks and months, I did indeed feel the mud rise. I felt the walk through the mud get harder and scarier. My confidence shook as I walked down the steep slope of that mud puddle. But the visual of the progress I was making gave me comfort and the courage to continue my walk. As Dr. Jill promised, the mud did rise to my waist and then my chest. I distinctly remember the moment the mud ultimately rose right underneath my nose, leaving me feeling as though with my next step, I would slip away into the mud entirely. But I could also very clearly feel the promise that with the next step, I would hit the incline and begin moving upward. That single visual gave me the courage and strength to take the next step and walk bravely to the long-awaited freedom from my mud puddle.

That time in my life gave way to many lessons and realizations, but potentially the biggest lesson I learned in all that strife was this:

The biggest blessings in my life usually look like the biggest disasters first.

I learned that the mud puddle isn't there to punish or destroy me; it's there to prepare me for the wonderful things waiting on the other side of the mud. I have to walk bravely through the mud to find the magic waiting for me. That life/God/the universe is always conspiring in my favor, but it often looks like a big hot mess first. That there is almost always something more wonderful than I could have dreamed up for myself on the other side, but the longer I stand at the foot of the mud puddle, the longer I will have to wait for that magic.

Mostly, I learned that the mud isn't something to fear. It is to be embraced, trusted, and appreciated. It can be hard to feel grateful for the mud when I am neck-deep in it, but it is what leads to the truly wonderful things in life. It's only when I realize the mud is my friend that I can walk through it with more acceptance and grace and get to the happiness waiting on the other side.

It took me a long time to realize my burnout was a mud puddle. I realized early on this was a lesson life was trying to teach me, but I failed to realize this enough-ness void was what I had been walking around for so long. My continued work would eventually lead me to realize how big this puddle was and how it would change me for the better. But at this point, I still had some mud to get through before all the pieces came together.

GOOD OR PURE MAGIC?

It's a long and incredibly random story as to how I became a *Grey's Anatomy* fan. As a person who does not, for the most part, enjoy things that are popular, I was adamantly against watching the show in its heyday. Along came a new friend, Courtney (How we met is another whole story that started with a boy, a boat dock, and the magical words, "When I dump him, I am keeping you." But I digress.), who invited me over for dinner after being astonished to find out I had never watched an episode of *Grey's*. She cooked me dinner and said in passing, "Oh, I just got the boxed set of *Grey's* in the mail today (this was 2010, remember life before Netflix?). Can we watch the first episode?"

As a person who was just happy someone else had cooked dinner, I said, "Sure, whatever you want works for me." She hit play and I was hooked from the first frame. One episode turned into two, and two turned into three, and three turned into a very late night. I dragged myself home and into bed knowing the alarm would be going off in only a few hours. That afternoon I called Courtney and said, "I am absolutely exhausted, but I need to watch more *Grey's*! Can I come over? I'll bring dinner!"

That night looked a lot like the night before—far more episodes than planned, a night later than was reasonable, and a very long following day. We repeated this pattern for the next few weeks (as I had eight or so seasons to catch up on) until eventually I just moved in with her so we could watch *Grey's* all night long and drink wine.

We spent an entire summer drinking wine, watching *Grey's*, talking about *Grey's*, pausing *Grey's* to share personal stories, quoting innumerable lines, arguing if Izzie was right or wrong for falling in love with Denny (To this day I adamantly contest that when love/infatuation is that strong, it's not a choice that you make consciously but something you get swept up in. Courtney disagrees with the same fervor.); discussing how even more than how attractive Derek Shepherd is, it's the way that he *looks* at Meredith that makes you swoon for him. It was a summer that gave me my best friend, shaped me, made me laugh, made me cry (so much crying), made me think, and made me love. Old *Grey's* was good. I mean really good.

Eventually, life took Courtney and me to different states, but we have always gravitated to the "good old days" of *Grey's* while half-heartedly watching the newer seasons. More than a few years later, Justin Chambers, who played Alex Karev, an original cast member, left the show. I had watched a lot less television and was more than a few episodes behind but decided to make it a priority to watch his departure before social media ruined the surprise of how he was written off the show.

I grabbed the remote, sunk into the couch and began watching the end of his story unfold. They sent Alex off in a way that focused on the beginning and tied his story neatly in a bow that only a fan of *Grey's* from the very beginning could appreciate and love (though to be fair, many didn't like it at all). As I started to watch, I cried. Feeling silly, I got myself together. But then the tears returned, and I cried some more. Eventually, I gave into the crying and began to appreciate the memories they put on screen, the reminder of the shared laughs and moments with my dear friend, the reminder of when *Grey's* made you cry almost every episode, when they made you feel something, relate to something or think differently about something. Upon wiping my tears, my first thought was, *That felt like old* Grey's. And, while there were a lot of old clips shown in the episode, it was more than that. It made you *feel* something. It made you connect.

Malcolm Gladwell has a podcast called *Revisionist History.* It's a magical podcast filled with thirty-minute episodes on all sorts of crazy topics, historical events, and random moments. A few weeks before watching Alex Karev leave *Grey's,* I had listened to an episode of the podcast called "McDonald's Broke My Heart." In this episode, Gladwell confesses his undying love of the McDonald's french fries of his youth: the crispy outside and the pillowy inside, the magic that was McDonald's fries. He shares the history of how the fries were created and served as the heart of the franchise. The fries were cooked originally in a specific type of fat that gave them their famed flavor. And the story of a man who believed that particular type of fat was very unhealthy and eventually led a nationwide charge against the fast-food giant to change the way the fries were made, resulting in the fries we know today. To prove that McDonald's french fries were better when cooked in the original fat, Gladwell then goes to extraordinary lengths to recreate the taste of the old fries. He rounds out the podcast with a taste test. Of course, the fries from the past won out with both Gen Xers and millennials.

He ends his podcast on a note about the bigger picture of what happened to McDonald's.

The original fries were sold in just one size. 2.4 ounces. You don't need any more fries than that. But nowadays, what's the large serving size of fries at McDonald's? 5.9 ounces. More than twice as big as it used to be. So, we've gone from the McDonald brothers' original product which gave us a modest amount of something sublime to a large amount of something that tastes like.[3]

As I heard the last remarks of his podcast while driving down the highway in Baltimore, I was struck deeply. He was right. Although I actually enjoy McDonald's french fries (fully admitting I am too young to have eaten McDonald's fries in the '70s, but only by a bit), the reality of his deeper sentiment hit home. We have moved from a modest amount of sublime to a large amount of something that taste like cardboard. It made me wonder how often in our lives we choose 5.9 ounces of something "just all right" instead of the 2.4 ounces of something magical?

As I sat processing my feelings about the *Grey's* episode I had just watched, Malcolm Gladwell's words came rushing back to me. How many *Grey's* episodes of late had I watched that were just okay? Episodes that were fine but paled in comparison to the *Grey's* of old that tugged at my heartstrings, left me with quotes I still find ways to work into conversation today, and made me debate morals with my best friend. I began to consider how often I was settling for 5.9 ounces of something just okay, instead of 2.4 ounces of something magical.

How many feelings and opportunities for real happiness and connection was I missing because of it? I vowed in that moment to leave behind 5.9 ounces and to start searching for 2.4 ounces of amazing.

That evening, it started simply enough with the television shows I had on my DVR that had become my weekly watching routine. As I sat and thought about the shows, I began to ask myself, "Are these really good? Like super good? Or are they just okay?" A week prior, I would have sworn they were great shows. I would have defended those few hours of TV watching over the course of the week as a valuable way to recharge my batteries at the end of a long day. But with this new litmus test, I had to objectively ask myself: Were they tugging at my heartstrings, making me think differently about the world, adding value into my life, leaving me with quotes on my heart for years to come, kind of sublime? Definitely not. Sadly, they were just good. Mindless good. Habit good. (All the shows on my DVR except *This Is Us,* because that, of course, *is* pure magic.)

So, in the commitment of living a life full of amazing, I deleted them. Because in order to be enveloped in the wonderful, you have to remove the just okay. How lucky to have found the same message in two very different places. *Grey's* and Gladwell, inspiring intentionality by indulging in 2.4 ounces of sublime.

CONSUMED BY THE DOING

As I continued to peel the layers away to rebuild my life in a more sustainable and meaningful way, my kids discovered the movie, *The Lorax.* As a parent who now spends many nights reading books to my children, I have come to love and admire how Dr. Seuss captures children's imagination by creating new worlds and made-up words. His ability to blend that creativity with deeper meanings and bigger lessons in a powerful way truly astounds me. So many of the messages that Dr. Seuss wrote about in this book in 1971 are still sadly applicable today. In *The Lorax*, Dr. Seuss tells the tale of greed and self-centeredness and the toll it has on the larger world.

As we sat cuddled on the couch while watching the movie, we

started discussing why the Once-ler was cutting down all the Truffula trees and why he felt it was okay to keep "biggering and biggering," even though it was hurting the animals around him. It was then I heard the Lorax ask the Once-ler the most profound question. "Which way does a tree fall?" To which the Once-ler confusingly answered, "Uh, down?" A wise and astute Lorax replied, "A tree falls the way it leans. Be careful which way you lean."[4]

The Lorax/Once-ler interaction passed over my children without much notice. But I spent the next twenty minutes thinking, which way did I lean? Was I even paying attention to which way I was leaning? I so often felt surrounded by the busyness and chaos of life. I was consumed by the doing that needed to be done, the movement from one thing to the next, and the energy it took to get it all done.

How long had I spent leaning into stress, chaos, unhappiness, busyness, guilt, and perfectionism? The reality was I had spent most of my life leaning into the chaos, chasing the busy, the doing and the accomplishing, yet somehow surprised when life felt chaotic. I was beginning to realize that I had much more to do with my own chaos than I had been aware. I became determined to pay much closer attention to which way I was leaning.

POPCORN AND BREAD BAGS

We are fortunate to live in a neighborhood with a lake. It's small but has a sandy beach and provides our family with hours of weekend fun in the sun during the summer. We are early risers in our house (Okay, the kids are early risers, and my husband and I have had to adapt), so we typically are out the door and headed to the beach around 8:30 or 9:00 a.m. The kids spend their days playing with friends at the shoreline, and the adults get a few minutes to sit in a chair and chat with friends while working on our tans. With two kids as little as ours, it's about as close to heaven as you can get on a weekend.

It was early on a Saturday morning a few weeks after *The Lorax* realization occurred. I was bustling around the kitchen, working to get the kids breakfast and the cooler packed so we could head to the beach.

As I opened the drawer to get bags for our PB&Js, I remembered we were out of bags. I could recap the story of what happened that morning, but my actual Facebook post below is far more telling of where I was in the slow but steady progress I was making on my journey.

(Imagine an incredibly messy junk drawer with empty sandwich bag boxes next to a picture of a smiling four-year- old on my lap happily eating popcorn out of a bread bag on the beach.)

"April, May, and June are aggressive in my line of work and our life shows it. Normally, about this time of year, I start beating myself up for all the things that are falling by the wayside. Because even though there's more on my plate than any person could actually manage, I somehow still expect flawless perfection of myself. Not only is it not possible, but the stress, anxiety, and yelling it causes clearly isn't healthy.

"I've been putting in the hard work to cut myself some slack, to forgive myself for what I can't do and to remember that being present and engaged in my life and with my family is more important than perfection in my household. Last week, we ran out of all our storage bags. Even the backups. And I immediately started beating myself up for not having been on top of that. However, I worked hard to remind myself that it's okay and not the end of the world. Then today, when packing food to take the kids to the lake, not having bags became an issue. I also didn't have much food to take for lunch. So, at 7:30 a.m. I threw on some clothes, jumped in the car, and headed to the store to buy bags and food. I knew it would make the morning more chaotic than it already was, and I could already hear myself barking at everyone when I got home to get in the car so we could get to the lake.

"In that moment, I stopped the car. I thought, Are bags and the perfect food for lunch really that important? Could you just go home and find a way to make lunch work, imperfect as it might be, so you can have a more peaceful morning and a more enjoyable day at the lake? Could, in this moment, you lower your expectations in order to make room for more time with the kids? Room for peace instead of chaos? Joy instead of perfection?

"I turned the car around and headed home. I used every last piece of bread we had in the house to make PB&Js and then used the bread bag to put our popcorn in.

"Did eating popcorn out of a bread bag have any impact on my kids? Not even a little.

"Did it make time for magical moments at the lake? Yes. Is it perfect? No.

"Is it something to be proud of? Definitely."

I so clearly remember being in the car as I exited our neighborhood. My anxiety was through the roof as I raced to the grocery store, my head flooded with the things I needed to buy. I was thinking through how long it would take me to get to the grocery store, shop, and return home and the timeline to then make food, pack, suntan lotion everyone and leave for the beach. I could feel my stress rising as I sped out of my neighborhood, when I remembered the words of the Lorax, "Be careful which way you lean." In that moment, it became painfully clear which way I was leaning. I was leaning into stress, I was leaning into perfectionism, I was leaning into creating my own chaos.

As I asked myself which way I wanted to lean, a picture of my kids flashed in my head. I saw a peaceful morning getting ready for the beach, I saw them walking down the hill with their boogie boards in hand, I saw myself sitting in a beach chair in the sun, I saw them playing in the water with their friends. I knew none of these things would happen if I continued to lean into the stress and chaos a morning trip to the grocery store would cause. I would arrive home full of adrenaline and groceries, chaotically getting food ready, leaving late, yelling at them to stand still as I threw sunscreen on them, and finally plopping into a beach chair fully frustrated and stressed out, grumbling about how busy life was. Catching myself in this act was a game changer for me…this was the moment to decide which way I wanted to lean.

I was so proud of myself for having made the right decision as I turned my car around to head back home. I walked into the kitchen and decided I would find a way to make it work. I really did use every last piece of bread in my house. I scrounged together chips, fruit, and some crackers I found in the back of the pantry. As I popped some popcorn (my son's favorite), I looked around the kitchen for a bag to put the popcorn in and laughed when I saw the empty bread bag. It made me smile as I shoved all the popcorn in the empty bag, because that simple act of imperfection represented how much progress I had already made on my journey.

I relished eating a PB&J on the beach made of two butt ends of a loaf of bread. And soaked in every minute of my daughter on my lap, eating a thrown-together lunch full of end-of-the-week leftovers. After months of soul searching and tears and self-discovery, it was the first time I felt like it was all starting to work. All the hard truths I was confronting and all the effort I was putting in finally felt like it was starting to pay off. I was beginning to believe that I could move past the perfectionism, the guilt, the need for validation, and the stress I had been leaning toward for so long. And then I sat back and soaked in some sun.

BRINGING THE BOARDROOM IN THE SHOWER

From the moment I became a mom, most days felt like I never stopped moving. The constant grind of all that needed to be done to keep my work and life afloat had a rhythm to it that was both comforting and exhausting. It was an unending switch between what was getting done and what needed to be done. My days were driven by my emails, my clients, my kids, my house, my schedule, and sometimes even my own chaos. Life was a whirlwind, moving from one task, conversation, training, activity, and to-do item to the next. As I began to work to change the whirlwind path I was on, I began to relish the experience of creating space in my life both mentally and physically. While the physical busyness of life was certainly a lot to manage, it became clear that more than anything, the mental busyness I was experiencing was the most taxing of all.

There didn't seem to be a single moment that I didn't have a thought running through my head about what needed to be done, where I needed to be, what I needed to take care of, and who needed something from me. Even after the emails were answered and the kids were put to bed, the running loop of stuff that bounced around my head was exhausting. When I wasn't doing what needed to be done or thinking about what needed to be done, I was mindlessly scrolling or watching or reading. There was a constant stream of input into my head. There was never a break—just noise.

When listening to an Oprah podcast one day, she discussed being present in the moment. Much like how often we hear about the importance of self-care, being present is a concept that gets a lot of attention these days. We are reminded how important it is to put our phones away, avoid mindless scrolling, enjoy the food we are eating instead of taking pictures of the plate. I worked hard to reduce my phone dependence and mindless scrolling (though some days even now, I still am better at this than others), but it didn't seem to give me the calm I was hoping to find.

But Oprah's guest, scientist Jon Kabat-Zinn said something that changed the way I thought about being present and unlocked the key to finding the peace and space I was after. "The next time you are in the shower, check to see if you are in the shower, because you may not be. Or you may have your whole Monday morning nine o'clock meeting in the shower with you."[5] While it was a laughable image at first, as the words sank in, it became clear how wise these words were.

Taking an exceptionally hot shower was and still remains one of my favorite parts of the day. With two kids under four years old at that point, most days it was the best chance I had at getting five minutes alone without anyone needing something from me. No matter what life was like only a few moments before, closing that shower curtain and turning on the steaming water was a much-needed timeout. Yet, if I were honest with myself, those five minutes weren't usually that peaceful. The first minute might be glorious, but soon after the mental to-do lists began taking shape. Even in my shower, there was a constant-ness that existed because I wasn't allowing for any second of time to go wasted. I thought about the way I had lived my days, and the constant-ness became alarming.

The minute my eyes opened in the morning, I thought about what hadn't been done, what needed to be done, and checked my email and calendar to see what I was missing. As I got dressed, I would check the weather, social media, my email (again), and log to-dos into my phone. As I made breakfast for the kids, I added Mickey Waffles to the grocery list on the counter while unloading the dishwasher. As I packed the kids' lunches and backpacks for school, I thought about spirit week next week and the 100 days T-shirts that still needed to be made. While driving to my first client appointment of the day, I listened to audiobooks and podcasts. While eating my lunch in my car between appointments, I scrolled through my phone, checking email and social media.

When I drove home, I called clients and listened to more audiobooks. When I got home, I checked my email again and made dinner, while thinking about the new presentation I needed to complete for next week's training. As I sat on the couch with the kids at the end of the night, I thought about all I had to get done once they were in bed. As we went through the bedtime routine, I thought about how I needed to purge the clothes that no longer fit them. As I walked out of their rooms and closed the door, I checked my email and then started cleaning up the house. As I sat on the couch, I grabbed my day planner to prep for the next day. As I put my planner away, I turned on the TV and usually fell directly asleep.

Constant motion. Constant planning. Constant mental input.

It became very clear that I had definitely been bringing the boardroom, along with everything else in my world, into my shower and into every other minute of my day. I was allowing the world, asking it even, to steal my five minutes of peace. There had to be a better way. There had to be a way to step into the shower and leave my worries and my to-dos on the other side of that curtain. Heck, if those plants needed five minutes, so did I! I needed to figure out how to soak in those glorious minutes of peace and quiet. If I could find a way to focus on five shower minutes of tranquility, maybe there was an opportunity to find even more.

I decided it was time to create some peace in my life. To put down the ever-spinning plates and create the room for some much-needed mental space so I could tune out the constantly-running to-do list. The mental peace to sit quietly and to absorb and let go of the day. The mental stillness to just *be*. However, knowing space was something I needed and knowing how to create it were two very different things. As a person so programmed for doing, stillness and space seemed both pretty "granola-y" and impossible. But I also knew the way I had been living my life wasn't working. I had been leaning toward the doing for so long it was time to shift my focus to establishing breathing room in my life.

ROCK. ROCK. ROCK

There were so many moments that stood out as turning points on my journey. So many big and small decisions that began to lay a new foundation for the kind of life I wanted to live. I was becoming more aware of how much I had been living on autopilot, how many unhealthy beliefs I held onto, and how much more control I had over how I lived my life than I had realized. It felt as though nearly every day I was peeling back a new layer of understanding of the lesson life was trying to teach me while giving me an opportunity to take a step in a better direction.

One particular day was much like any other, except it was a day that my son was having a hard afternoon. He was in the transition period that happens just before dropping an afternoon nap. That rough time period where if he napped, he was up all night (and subsequently, so was I), but if he didn't nap, our afternoons were rough as he was super crabby. That afternoon everything set him off. Everything was a fight with his sister. Everything ended in a complete meltdown. It was clear he needed a nap. It was also clear that it was too late in the day for him to take one with any hope of either of us sleeping that night. After spending much of the afternoon yelling and being frustrated with his behavior, I decided there had to be a better way. Instead of leaning toward the frustration, I decided it was time to stop fighting and instead to call a mommy-and-son timeout.

"Do you want to do some rocking?" I asked him.

"Yes, please," he said through tears and we headed up to his room.

The rocking chair in his room is one we bought before my daughter was born. It's big, gray, not very attractive, but super comfy. I have rocked both babies to sleep in that chair, soothed them in that chair, read books with both kids on my lap in that chair. And though it takes up way too much space in his small room, I can't bring myself to get rid of it. I know there are only so many more snuggle sessions I will get with them, and I don't want to miss a single one for the sake of more floor space. (A few days earlier, as I was huffing about how there wasn't any space for his toys in his room, my husband suggested that getting rid of the chair would give us the space we needed, and I burst into tears. So, yeah, we are keeping the chair a bit longer.)

As I walked into his room and sat in the rocker, he grabbed his favorite blanket and crawled up on my lap. I started rocking as he laid his head on my chest and let out that deep sigh only babies being comforted by their moms have. I placed my cheek against the top of his head, and for two entire minutes, I soaked in all the bliss I could as the entire world slipped away and we rocked.

Somewhere around the three-minute mark, it happened though. The load of laundry I had started two hours ago entered my thoughts.

Dang it. I need to switch that load of laundry and get the sheets dried before bed.

I paused. Rock, rock.

I can't forget to do that. I'll do it when we get up.

Another pause. Rock, rock, rock.

Then the proposal I needed to send out to my client raced through my head.

Shoot. I didn't get that proposal finished. I need to send that out before the end of the day. I wonder if I can send details of the program in an email or if they need something more formal.

Rock, rock, rock, rock.
I was on autopilot, running through the list of to-dos.

But just then, he snuggled in deeper, his head nuzzling against my cheek and his sweet, deep sigh snapped me back to the moment.

What am I doing? Why am I thinking about laundry and proposals when I have this moment of bliss cuddled in my lap? How many more times will he let me do this with him? I am TOTALLY bringing the boardroom in the shower! I scolded myself.

It was time to be present in the moment. I took a breath, closed my eyes, and nuzzled his little head back. I let go of the to-do list running through my head and rocked lovingly with him in that chair, leaving the boardroom where it belonged. It was my first step in creating enough mental space to truly connect, and that clarity came while I got to enjoy a magical moment with my snuggly little boy.

SEVENTEEN BEACH TOWELS

I love a good audiobook. They help me learn through others, process things differently, and often help me see situations or realities in my own life differently. As I listened to the words of a story by Joshua Becker while driving to DC, I was struck by the reality of a dad's inter-action with his son. Joshua was determined to clean the garage, but his son wanted to play. After shooing his son away so he could finish cleaning the garage, he felt guilt tug at his heartstrings.[6]

A beautiful day, a kid desperate to play, and a dad who wanted to, but a garage full of stuff pulling at him to be sorted, cleaned, and orga-nized. I could so clearly see myself in this scenario, standing in my garage, being pulled by the "should" of having a clean and organized garage and the opposite "should" of spending time with my kids.

Playing with the kids was clearly the right option, but there was just so much other housework to be done.

I felt this pull frequently. The pull of wanting to be the mom who played with her kids and created great memories, but also the mom who had a house that felt peaceful and calm. I wanted to spend time engaging with my kids while having a house where things were organized and easy to access. But with a full-time job and two little kids, there never seemed enough time to do either of those things, let alone both. The worst part was, no matter which option I chose, I always felt guilty about the option I didn't choose. As I listened to the audiobook and heard the man share his story about a beautiful day spent cleaning a garage, I could feel the guilt that always weighed on me as I walked past our garage door, because ours, too, was in desperate need of an overhaul. Before I knew it, I got sucked into thinking of all the things that needed an organizational facelift in my house: the linen closet, the kitchen cabinets, my dresser drawers, the bathroom cabinets. The list went on and on. There was a nearly constant pull on my mind to the spaces that needed my attention and time. It all needed to be done and it all felt important, but there just wasn't enough time to get everything done. It was a constant reminder that I wasn't trying hard enough (after all, a Good Mom would have perfectly organized closets and cabinets), and I wasn't doing enough.

I snapped myself out of the shame spiral I was headed down and brought myself back to the audiobook. Over the course of the next few hours, I heard the story unfold of a family who lived with the same pull I felt but instead of constantly cleaning and organizing, decided to instead declutter. The narrator spoke about how reducing the items in their house gave them back more time as a family because they were no longer shuffling, organizing, and cleaning the massive number of things they had. He told of a house that felt more peaceful and allowed them to spend their time together as a family, instead of constantly moving from household chore to household chore. He shared that they had erased their family debt with the money they saved and finally had money in their savings account.

The vague idea I had of minimalism was of a house with no furniture, white pictureless walls, three spoons in a barren kitchen drawer, and one pair of shoes in the bottom of an empty closet. As I listened, however, an entirely new picture was painted for me: afternoons spent playing with the kids, a kitchen with space in each cabinet, clothes that I loved in closets with enough room to actually see them, a garage with enough space for the kids' bikes and scooters to ensure I didn't nearly kill myself every time I pulled them out. I began to buy into the idea that instead of cleaning and organizing more, we simply needed to have less.

"That's it," I said to myself. "It's time to clean things out. I'm tackling the linen closet tonight." I knew there were some towels that could be purged and some extra toiletries that could be donated to create space and make it more "minimal."

The whole day I was excited to get home and start purging. The second the kids were in bed, I raced to the linen closet and dumped the entire contents onto the living room floor. Because true to how I live my life, the only way I know how to fix or clean anything is to dump it all out and start reorganizing and rebuilding from scratch. As I gazed upon the heaping piles that surrounded me, I realized how severely I had underestimated what was in that closet. I knew there was a lot, but man, there was a LOT! It appeared as though I confused preparedness with borderline hoarding. Much to my shock, I had over one hundred tiny bottles of shampoos, conditioners, body washes, suntan lotions, hand sanitizers, and face scrubs. One hundred!

I sat on the floor organizing these giant mounds of toiletries into "Keep," "Donate," and "Pitch." As I waded through the sea of stuff, I began to wonder why I had so many items shoved into that tiny closet. I had never had a need for even a quarter of the items, and I couldn't imagine when I would ever need them, especially in that quantity. Why had I been shoving all these things in my linen closet, organizing, reorganizing, buying new storage bins, rearranging shelves, berating myself for it not being perfectly organized (because when there are that many things in a closet, it's nearly impossible to keep it organized), but never stopping to ask myself why I had so much stuff in the first place?

As I continued sorting, I exasperatedly wondered aloud to my husband, "Why in the world do we have seventy-seven bottles of travel-sized shampoos, conditioners, and body washes? When would we *ever* need this much shampoo? Why have I been shoving so many things we don't need into our closets?"

No wonder going into that closet was always such a source of stress. Every time I opened it, the clutter unnerved me, and the amount of time and effort it took to find anything in there was exhausting. And on top of it all, it made me feel like a slob for having a closet in the shape that it was.

I decided to keep a small basket of travel items (as I do travel for work and tiny hairsprays are much easier to pack), a small basket for suntan lotions and bug sprays, and one small basket for first-aid necessities. Leaving me with two full bags to donate to our local homeless shelter.

Next, I headed to the towels. As I began gathering the towels from the floor to refold and put them all back on the shelves, I looked down at how many towels I had. Twenty-three. I had twenty-three bath towels. "Who needs twenty-three bath towels?" I shouted into the air at no one in particular. Eight. I was going to keep eight towels, and the rest went into the donate pile.

I was on a roll and loving the adrenaline rush I was getting from minimizing my life. On to the beach towels. Seventeen! "WHY DO WE HAVE SEVENTEEN BEACH TOWELS?" I was closer to yelling at this point. Seventeen beach towels all fighting each other for space on a shelf far too small to hold ten beach towels, let alone seventeen. No wonder they were always crammed in there, needing to be refolded and reshoved back onto the shelf every time I put a towel away.

It took me a few hours that evening to purge, sort, box up, and reorganize the items from the closet. During that time, the questions why? and how much? kept running through my head. Why did I have all this stuff and how much time, energy, and peace of mind had been robbed by dealing with all these things over the past few years?

As I gathered the items to donate to the homeless shelter, I felt a wave of panic. What if I got rid of these towels and we had a houseful of people and I didn't have enough towels for them all? What if someone came to our house and they needed travel shampoo for a trip? (Please don't ask me how or why this would ever actually happen, as now it seems ridiculous to even imagine. At the time however, the concern was real.) If I donated all this, if I kept only the minimal amount of what I needed, maybe I wouldn't have what someone needed, and I would miss an opportunity to be the hero.

In a flash, I had my answer. I had been keeping all these items to ensure I could take care of other people and feel needed.

I walked through my house, opening drawers and cabinets, all of them stuffed to the brim, mostly organized but completely stuffed. There wasn't an ounce of breathing room in any of them. I opened every kitchen cabinet and looked at them all with a new set of eyes. Between wine glasses, coffee cups, water glasses, kid cups, and beer glasses, we easily had a hundred. How many things was I holding onto for the sake of others?

Opening my closets, I realized each were crammed full of clothes I hardly ever wore and some I didn't even like. The top of my closet was stuffed with items that didn't have a place anywhere else in the house, so they got tossed up there "just in case" I ever needed them. My bathroom cabinets overflowed with shampoo, nail polish remover, shaving cream, toothpaste. Who needs seven backup toothpastes? I had dozens and dozens of pairs of socks in my dresser drawer, so many that I had to smash them down to get it to close.

"I don't think I am enough," I whispered to myself. I let the reality of that statement sit for a moment. It had been there the whole time, making itself known in every overflowing cabinet and overstuffed drawer—my enough-ness void. Never feeling good enough, always needing to be prepared to take care of others so they would see me as valuable and fill my enough-ness tank. The void had manifested itself in a house overflowing with things. Until that day, I had been unable to see how all the pieces were connected.

It suddenly all fit together perfectly. The perfectionism, the striving for approval, the working myself to the bone looking for validation from myself and from others, the inability to feel content in my decisions, sacrificing so much of myself in hopes others would see me as giving and selfless, the constant comparison, the excessive guilt, filling each drawer, cabinet and shelf to the brim just in case someone needed something. It all came crashing together. I had never seen what these all had in common before.

"I don't think I am enough." I said again, this time a little louder. As the pieces continued to connect. I now saw the perfectionism, the need for external validation, the frustration when my hard work didn't feel noticed, the guilt I walked around in all the time, the flurry of activity trying to do it all and be all for everyone, the momentary high of recognition and the constant chasing of appreciation for what it really was. I had spent my whole life chasing enough-ness. Always looking for it from others, frustrated when they couldn't fill that tank for me.

As I continued to soak in this new revelation, it became clear the path I had taken was never going to work. It seemed so obvious. No one could *ever* fill my enough-ness tank, not a friend, partner, parent, or child. There was no amount of approval or gratitude they could give that would fill that void. And there was certainly no accomplishment or level of perfection that could fill it. It was up to me to find it for myself. I was the only one who could ever make myself feel whole and worthy. To finally feel enough. And that's when it hit me, there was no need to find a way to fill it because I was *enough already.* Because you don't earn enough-ness; you just are.

I would love to say that this flash of clarity came like it does in a movie, with a few chance happenings and the world spinning around the character, while a montage with emotional music makes everything instantly clear. But the reality is that it was a culmination of all the work I had been doing on myself for the previous few months that laid the foundation for this moment. I had been working so dili- gently on myself, nudging myself along with no real understanding of where I was headed other than the belief that if I just kept walking through the mud, the answers would come. I hadn't connected the dots. I wasn't aware I was standing in the middle of a mud puddle, but sure enough, in that moment, that too became clear.

The whole journey had been a mud puddle. Life had given me so many opportunities to walk through this mud puddle, but I never did. I'm not even sure I was paying enough attention to realize there even was one there. I had not acknowledged the mud. I was too obstinate and scared to see it, let alone walk through it. I hadn't made the slow, intentional, brave walk in from my ankles to my knees, waist, and chest. Life had given me those opportunities before, but I had turned and walked away from the mud. So, after numerous attempts to lead me to the mud with no success, life threw me in, right there into the middle of the puddle. Life had a lesson to teach and there was no avoiding it.

So, that day in the kitchen when it all came crashing down around me, life picked me up by the seat of my pants and threw me in head-first. Thankfully, I was smart enough at the time to know that the only way out of the situation was to walk the rest of the way. And what I had been experiencing over the previous weeks and months was the continued push through the mud. Every step was another piece. Every small "aha" moment was another few inches through the mud.

And true to my experience with life and mud puddles, better things than I could have ever imagined waited for me on the other side: an understanding of the void, a knowing that I am enough just by being, a clarity of the habits and beliefs I had been carrying around that kept me living a stressful and unsustainable lifestyle, a contentment in a way I had never known, and a genuine connection and happiness. I felt like Dorothy in *The Wizard of Oz* who realized that she had the power to go home the whole time. I had the power to believe differently, to behave differently, to feel differently all within myself. It wasn't until I was in the mud and felt the void that I realized only I could fill it.

I spent the next few nights going through every closet, cabinet, and drawer in my house. I worked hard to look realistically at the things I had in each space and to reduce those items to only what I truly needed or really, really loved. I just knew I needed more space to breathe, less time feeling chaotic, and more energy to spend on things I enjoyed instead of managing items in the house.

With each item I let go of, I had a deeper understanding of my enough-ness void and how it had been impacting my life. It became clear just how much I had been tolerating and inviting into my life in order to feel a sense of enough-ness. I didn't know how I was going to fill my enough-ness tank, but I was proud that I had walked far enough through the mud to know this was the core of my struggle. I had reached the bottom of my mud puddle, and now it was time to start climbing out the other side.

As I continued to purge my house, confront my demons, and connect more to minimalism, I began to realize that at its core, minimalism isn't about a lack of possessions. It is about carefully considering what you have and only allowing what adds value to it. Since that first heavy purge, I have done a few more rounds, paring things down even further. If you looked at my house today, you probably wouldn't think it was inspired from a minimalism framework. I still have more things than could probably be considered truly minimalistic (I mean, I still have two kids and way more Christmas decorations in my crawl space than a human being should have), but I have let go of all the things I was hanging on to for the "just in case" moments. The things that were stealing my time and my energy and were simply an attempt to fill my enough-ness void. I am proud to say that the things I have in my house now are for me and my family.

Even more strikingly, I have realized that minimalism shares many things in common with the values I learned on my journey. Minimalism is about being careful which way you lean. It's about having 2.4 ounces of sublime instead of 5.9 ounces of cardboard. It's about creating space to breathe and feel peace. But mostly, it's about realizing that you already have and are enough.

RUNNING AT THEIR PACE, NOT MINE

I threw my carry-on under the seat in front of me, sat down, closed my eyes, and took a deep breath. I had two hours' worth of work to complete on this flight, but it was 6:50 a.m. and I needed a second. A few minutes later, I opened my eyes and looked at the passenger on my left, wondering who else was crazy enough to be up this early heading to Orlando. I was off to a training that started that afternoon. My business partner had graciously flown in the night before to lighten the number of nights I would be gone and help me maintain some "work/life harmony" as we call it.

The sweet woman two seats away glanced over at me and smiled. As I bent down to grab my laptop out of my carry-on, I said, "Are you heading out this early for work or for fun?" She explained she was heading to Disney for the Princess Half-Marathon. Over the course of the next two hours, we chatted about everything imaginable: work, family, houses (as it turns out we lived within ten minutes of each other), kids, and eventually the conversation turned back to her half-marathon.

She began describing how she had just started running a few years earlier and this was only her second half-marathon. She was nervous but felt more prepared because of her first marathon experience. She described having trained well for the first race and felt ready from an endurance and fitness perspective. But the one thing she had not prepared for was running with other runners.

"I struggled in my first half-marathon because for much of the race I found myself running next to other runners and ended up running at their pace and not mine. As I hadn't been running very long, I didn't know the cadence of my own stride and overextended myself much too early in the race and ran out of steam. The last half of the marathon was painful, and I could barely get myself through it. At the end I felt defeated and exhausted."

She went on to describe the last 5K she ran—how she was much more intentional about finding her own cadence and how much better she felt about her run when she was done.

"I just have to remember to run at my own pace and not get caught up in the pace of those running around me. If I can do that, I will be just fine."

I was struck by the power of her words. It made me think back about my life and wonder how much of the stress and struggle I had faced was because I was trying to run at a pace that wasn't right for me. How often had I used the cadence of others to judge my own race? How frequently had I been running too fast or too slow because of the pace of those around me, or because I was running at a pace I thought I *should* be running instead of a natural fit for me? I could see that for a long time I had been running at everyone else's pace, but these last few months had been about working to find my own pace.

As we started our descent and wrapped up our conversation, I settled into my seat. I hadn't done an ounce of the work waiting for me, but I had engaged in an incredibly insightful and meaningful conversation with a super sweet woman. In that small window of time, her story and words had helped me realize that I was beginning to hit my own stride. I was finding the cadence to my own race, and what was important now was staying true to that pace.

BACK TO THE BEACH

As the year pressed on, it was time to head back to Nags Head for our family vacation. I was excited to get my toes back in the sand and find some space for mental clarity. Our weeks at the beach have always been enjoyable and relaxing, but as I continued my enough-ness journey, I began to recognize the space the beach week created for me. It was a time for reflection and recalibration. This year, I was more intentional about taking the week to pause and listen to the lessons life was trying to show me.

I was dedicated to getting some alone time in the morning to walk the beach and just be. I made space for sunrises and sunsets, something I had always loved but was finding more and more peace in. One morning as I walked the beach, I began reflecting on the past year. I was getting more comfortable in asking for what I needed and setting boundaries against guilt around self-care activities. That year at the beach was the first time I had ever taken an alone morning since having the kids, and it was magic.

One morning I did beach yoga, another I sat and cross-stitched on the deck. That was the beginning of the period in my life when I spent a lot of time working my way through potential undiscovered self-care habits, including but not limited to cross-stitching (fairly soothing but only in easy patterns with limited colors where I could zone out instead of doing too much math!), knitting (more enjoyable than I had planned but again…math), acupuncture (just okay, I really thought I would enjoy it more than I did), and floating in a float tank (shockingly fantastic, as I assumed I would be freaked out floating in the dark, but it was amazing and I would go every day if I could).

I worked so hard that vacation to slow my mind and quiet my heart and truly just be. Each day I could feel myself settling further and further into peacefulness. It was as though my entire being felt differently on that trip. A switch had flipped, and it became clear that I wanted that peace and tranquility not just on vacation, but in my everyday life too.

During that week, everything seemed so clear. It was easy to recognize what things were important in life, how much better I felt when I didn't let external factors run my emotions, and how much happier I was when I took life as it came instead of working so hard to run it over.

The last morning of vacation, I went for an early morning sunrise walk on the beach. I remember fighting desperately to soak in every minute of peace I felt near the ocean. I was willing time to stop, even just for a few minutes so I could savor the tranquility of the waves crashing on the shore and the feel of sand underneath my feet. I couldn't ever remember a time where I had felt so peaceful. The weight of the next day's return home sat heavy in me. I was trying to bottle up the peace from that morning and lock it in my soul, so that back in reality, I could tap into that peace once again.

As I walked, I came across a beautiful wooden pier that stretched out a hundred yards into the ocean. The sun was just rising above the horizon, and it lit the sky up in the brightest orange and pink explosion I had ever seen. I stood there, listening to the waves and soaking in the tranquility and beauty of the moment. This was the moment I wanted to be able to tap into when I was at home. This sense of peace and connectedness had to be something that existed in moments other than during beach walks one week out of every year. I grabbed my phone and took a picture of the pier, the sky, and the waves. I continued to walk and watched the sun turn every shade of pink, red, and finally blue. It was time to head back to the beach house. I took one final deep breath, determined to hold tight to the slowness and peacefulness I felt in that moment.

Upon returning to the beach house, I immediately made the picture I had taken at the pier the wallpaper on my phone, hoping it would be a daily reminder of how I wanted to feel more often. I had been doing a better job managing my life, but the next part of my journey wasn't just about surviving my life—it was about enjoying and connecting to it.

Of course, as usually is the case, even with my newfound determination, nearly as soon as the car left the beach house driveway, I could feel the peace and tranquility slipping away. I fought it, I begged it to stay, but within a day or two, I was back to square one with only the distant memory of the tranquility I had hoped would remain.

Nearly every vacation I have ever gone on, I have had the same experience. I feel peaceful and calm and connected to myself, only to come home and almost instantly lose the feeling and wait for the following year's vacation to experience it again. But here is where the story takes a turn. This year was different. Perhaps because of all the work I had been putting in or the changes I was already making, but I became unwavering in finding a way to feel peace and connection to myself throughout the year, not just while walking the beach on vacation. To prioritize connectedness and happiness just as much as I prioritized doing and accomplishing.

It began slowly, with a quiet determination to carve out space for peace in my days. And over the next few years, with a lot of attention and determination, it came to fruition.

THE SHIFT

As I share my story of burnout and the deep need for external valida-tion with women across the country, it becomes clear that I am not alone in this battle for enough-ness. Others' stories have different circumstances, different root causes, and different paths, but there is a commonality that runs deep around this idea. The single biggest ques-tion I get asked when sharing my journey is, what did you do and how can I do it too? If you are still reading this and my story has resonated with you in some way, you are likely looking for the "how to" to get to the other side. I share the last half of this book, not as instructions, but rather as the truth in my path in hopes that some of the changes I made may help you as well.

What I can tell you is that the positive changes were more subtle than the demise. Remembering the pivotal, life-changing moments of my discovery journey is easy. They will forever be burned in my brain as the moments where the realization of my unhealthy beliefs became clear. What aren't as shining are the tiny moments, the subtle shifts in behavior, the slow grinding of a different path. So often in life we are looking for the big moment, the turning point, the "new and improved." But real change has come from realizing these truths and then making steady and consistent behavior changes that support the new life I want to lead.

Sure, along the way there were big moments that affirmed the new life I was leading, but it's the everyday, uncelebrated, quiet moments and decisions that I chose that make the real difference. I will do my best to share both the big moments and the small ones that have helped me stand firmly in my enough-ness in hopes that you, too, will have the courage to make the right decisions for yourself.

SLOWLY, THEN ALL AT ONCE

I started following Jenna Fischer (Pam, from *The Office*) on Instagram, and she had recently gotten into bread making. I mean *deep* into bread making. Every Instagram story was fifteen sections long as she made bread, talked about bread, asked questions about bread, ate bread, and then continued to talk more about bread. This went on for months. You could see how much she genuinely enjoyed bread making, and it seemed clear that her bread was fantastic.

Then one night, my husband and I watched a cooking documentary show on Netflix: *Salt, Fat, Acid, Heat*. In the show, they broke down food to its most basic and fundamental aspects. During one episode, they discussed how food has changed over the decades, moving from food that we make from scratch to the highly processed foods that we so often find ourselves reaching for now. Not just chips and candy but the fundamental foods of bread, meat, sauces, dressings, and so on. Although this wasn't a new idea to me, the way they spoke about what we are missing in the enjoyment of making and the taste of homemade food really gave me pause. Was this another moment settling for good enough when I could be experiencing magic?

I had been toying with the idea of making my own bread, but the food documentary pushed me over the edge. I found a white bread recipe online that required kneading, because if you are going to take on bread making, you want to get the full experience. Since then, I've found that a no-knead recipe can be just as tasty, and I make those frequently now, but I wanted the full bread-making experience at the time.

So, one Sunday afternoon, I grabbed flour, yeast, salt, and water and got to work. I had no idea what I was doing but figured I couldn't mess up bread making *that* badly. I spent the next few hours tending to my loaf. Measuring (I would later learn that "real" bread recipes recommend weighing ingredients, but for this recipe and for many that I still use, measuring works well enough), activating, waiting, combining, waiting, kneading, waiting, and baking (more waiting!). It was time consuming to make homemade bread. And let me tell you, it did not disappoint.

I will never forget the first loaves I pulled out of the oven. Even as two simple, plain-white loaves of bread, it was life changing. I took them out of the bread pan, let them cool as long as I could (because I was *dying* to eat some), cut a slice for my husband and myself, slathered a glob of butter on each piece and trotted into the living room where I sat on the couch next to my husband and we took our first bite of heaven. To try and describe how much better homemade bread is than store-bought bread is nearly impossible, but it is—it really, really is.

That day changed the way I thought about my family's relationship with food. We had always eaten what I considered healthy, but I began to see all the places where I allowed big companies to make my food. From that point since, I have worked hard to make as much as I can from scratch, not because I needed to in order to be a Good Mom but because I wanted to make the change for my family. But I digress. Back to the bread.

In the years since, I have made hundreds of loaves of bread. I have made loaves standing in our kitchen, lovingly kneading bread when I was stressed out and needed some solace. I have made bread multiple times in a week for our family because it's the only kind of bread my daughter would (and still will) eat. I have made bread to give away to family and friends. I have made bread over FaceTime with my mom when she ran out of the bread I had sent back with her to Michigan after her last visit and when we were missing each other during the pandemic. I have taught friends and I have been taught by friends.

Without question, making bread has been 2.4 ounces of glorious, not just from the highly superior taste of the bread itself, but even more so in the joy that making bread has brought to my life. There is something magical about getting out the ingredients and preparing to make something I know my family enjoys so much. I love the time it takes to make the bread. In a time when so much of what we encounter is instantaneous and available at the touch of a finger (or a phone), I love spending time creating something so wonderful that won't be rushed. It can't be coaxed or convinced to rise faster or to bake more speedily than it needs to. It requires both attention and patience. But its reward is something greater than can be purchased.

Normally when making bread, I set a timer for the ten minutes it takes for the yeast to bloom, and I take care of some other chore that requires my attention. I walk away from a bowl of warm water and yeast, only to return ten minutes later to a layer of activated, frothy goodness waiting to be combined with flour and salt. It's pretty cool.

One afternoon, I felt impatient because I was in a hurry. I walked past the bowl about eight minutes in and the yeast had not yet bloomed. I stared into a cloudy bowl of water, disappointed and wondering if the yeast was bad or if I had killed it with water that was too hot. While looking at the water, I began to see a pop of yeast froth to the top. Realizing that I had never seen the yeast actually bloom before, I stood there to wait for more. One more pop of yeast bloomed. Then another. What followed was nothing short of shocking. In the next seven seconds, the entire bowl exploded with yeast bloom. It popped up from under the cloudy water and came bursting to life with fervor. It was all there under the surface just waiting to explode, and just like that, all at once, it did.

The change in my life since hitting burnout has felt a lot like the yeast bloom that day. At first, the lessons were sporadic. They came slowly as I processed each one and worked through its meaning and application in my life. A pop here and a pop there. Then the lessons gained speed as I became more comfortable hearing the messages and implementing change in my life. I gained speed as I began to grow more confident in myself, feeling the change as healthier tapes played in my head and connecting to the joy that came when I moved past the guilt that had plagued me so deeply. I was settling into enough-ness. I began to see clearly when I was making a decision or feeling a certain pain because of old habits trying to fill the enough-ness void. I would then consciously choose the decision that was in line with the new life I wanted to lead.

Then one day it happened. I remember standing in my bedroom getting ready for a busy day. I only had a few minutes to get showered, dressed, and get on the road. I saw a pile of folded clothes at the end of the bed, making a mental note to put them away when I got home from work, and I finished getting ready.

All of a sudden, I stopped in my tracks. This simple thought, to put away my clothes when I got home from work, did not make me instantly connect to worrying about the state of my house, chores that needed to be done, or how a Good Mom's bedroom looks. It was void of judgment, guilt, and shame. I stood in my bedroom with my head wildly spinning, no longer thinking about getting myself out the door. When had this thought, the one void of judgment and guilt become my default? Were all my thoughts this free of judgment and guilt? Were they all able to so easily detach those external things from my worthiness and enough-ness? Those thoughts, those judgmental, unforgiving tapes that had lived in my mind for so long; it was shocking to realize they hadn't played when I looked at that pile of folded clothes at the foot of my bed.

Had I done it? Had I truly changed the beliefs that had been unrelenting for so long? I stood there and, in that moment, I could feel the enough-ness. I could sense the scales had tipped. The weight of feeling enough in my own skin was heavier than the insecurity, the need for validation, and the guilt. I could clearly see the habits and the tapes that no longer served me. I could sense the shift that had occurred, slowly and then all at once. I brought myself back to the moment, feeling different than I had just a few minutes before: proud, aware, empowered, and grateful.

The truth is that of course I had not "arrived." There is no arriving. But I had settled into a new normal, a new set of eyes through which to make decisions. I continued to rush around getting myself ready to head out the door, now sure I could handle whatever waited for me on the other side.

ALL WITHIN OURSELVES

Let me be clear. This newfound clarity was not an immediate pass to being a fully whole human who doesn't have insecurities, guilt, and places to continue growing. But I have reached a place where I can recognize when an unhealthy tape sneaks back in and can now take it out and put a better, healthier one in. I can look objectively at guilt I am experiencing and ask myself, "Are you feeling this guilt because of unrealistic expectations you are putting on yourself or because something is truly out of whack in your life and you need to work to get things in balance?" I can see places where my thoughts are hindering my growth, progress, and happiness and opt to look at the situation differently.

That is not to say I am walking around in a state of bliss and am no longer an overachieving, full-go, pedal-to-the- metal, sometimes burning-the-candle-at-both-ends, type A. Because I definitely am. The difference is that I no longer do those things because I am hoping someone else will notice and validate me. I do them because that is how I am wired.

I like running at full speed. I like the heavy load that I can carry. I like pushing myself to accomplish all that I can. I am energized by working hard all day and crawling into bed feeling like I gave it all I had. The difference is that I used to do all those things with the weight of guilt and my own (and perceived societal) expectations, and sadness and frustration when I didn't get the validation I was so desperately seeking. Now I do them because they make me feel good and alive and happy and proud.

From the outside, things probably don't look like they've changed that much. If you were to ask my friends and family, my guess is they would not be able to pinpoint much difference in who I was pre-burnout and who I am now. Externally, my drive, what I enjoy and how I spend my days, probably looks close enough to the same as before. I doubt anyone would be able to detect the life-altering experience I went through. But that may be the biggest indicator to me as to just how far I have come.

You see, beforehand, that would have bothered me. I would have wanted people to see the work I put in. To know they saw the difference from where I was to where I had grown and were proud of me in having done the work and gotten the result. But that would have been the enough-ness void talking. I truly, wholeheartedly, and gratefully am happy to allow the changes I have made, to be enough, just for me. Because it means I didn't have to change everything about myself to become a happier person. I just needed to settle into the person I already was. Because I was already enough. I was just the only one who didn't know it.

I think this is true for so many of us. We carry around this belief that we are somehow "less than" and everyone else has it all together. We give external forces so much power over how we feel about ourselves. We allow the precious days we have on this earth to be spent feeling worried, sad, unworthy, and many times unlovable over trivial and often superficial things. We wait unhappily for external forces to change, to get better, or to be fixed in hopes that when they do, we will feel better about ourselves and our lives. When in reality, we are much like Dorothy in *The Wizard of Oz*. We have the power to make things better, all within ourselves.

EXTREMES

I am good at discipline, extreme discipline: eating healthy, exercising, taking my vitamins, organizing my house, planning, going to bed early, and waking up early. At least for a while. Inevitably, however, there is always a swing back to the other extreme. After too much discipline, I end up eating everything in sight, staying up late, waking up late, and spending my day reacting to all the things coming at me. These are two extremes I have spent most of my life oscillating between.

It's taken me a long time and a lot of soul searching to understand this pattern and where it comes from. It's become clear that it's easy to feel enough in the moment when I am super organized, a clean freak, and incredibly disciplined with planning my day. But to maintain that level of discipline and effort, I end up exhausted and screaming at my family for every dropped sock, crumb on the counter, and dirty plate in the sink. Which ultimately leaves me feeling terrible about how I am interacting with my family. So, I swing totally the other way. I give up on being perfect and stop planning my days, stop worrying about the house being clean, and let toys pile up in bedrooms and clothes in drawers run amok. Then I get tired of living haphazardly and swing back to perfection.

The struggle for me had always been recognizing when I was in an extreme and how that negatively impacted my life. Extremes always ended up being behaviors that were not mentally or physically sustainable. No matter which extreme the behavior fell, I always ended in exhaustion from the energy it took to live there.

You may ask, why then did I live in the extreme instead of the middle? Because while extremes can be exhausting, in some ways, they are also easier. They are comfortable, easy to define, and typically fairly achievable for a short time. It's easy to know what a perfectly clean house looks like, no matter the cost. It's easy to know what exercising every day looks like, regardless of how tired my body or mind might be. It's easy to know what foods are the right ones to choose when eating extremely healthy.

And it's also easy to know what a messy house looks like, regardless of the stress a messy house might cause. It's easy to eat whatever I want paying no attention to its healthfulness. It's easy to ignore the tennis shoes sitting under the exercise bike in my basement when I never even consider working out.

What isn't easy is figuring out how clean "clean enough" is. If it isn't perfectly clean or totally messy, how do I know if it's the right balance between unreasonable, perfectly clean and a complete mess? How much exercise in a week is enough to get me in the shape I want to be in versus taking enough downtime to recharge my batteries? What foods can I treat myself to without them affecting my waistline? How much planning is enough to have a good and productive day but doesn't result in yelling at my kids because they are taking forever and it's messing up my to-the-minute schedule? How do I work enough to give it my all without spending all my days and nights grinding myself into the ground and missing out on important family time? How do I know if I'm doing it right or if it's good enough if I'm not seeking perfection?

These are the questions that have plagued me for a lifetime. How do I find a middle without letting the uncertainty that inevitably comes from being in the middle rule my life? Am I doing enough? Am I doing too much? Am I doing too little? It was easier to live in the exhaustion of the extreme than to live in the exhaustion of constantly judging and questioning myself about every decision.

I have spent most of my adult life trying to find a middle, a balance, some harmony. To feel accomplished and successful operating in the middle. Because even when I set an ideal middle, there was always that little nagging voice that said I should be doing more, working harder, struggling more, digging deeper. That in order to succeed, to be accomplished, to finally feel "enough," I needed to do a little more than I had done. Then there was the bigger concern of picking the wrong middle. What if what I picked was too much of one thing and not enough of another? Feeling enough has always been just out of reach.

It turns out it was my enough-ness void that demanded extremes. It required a right and a wrong, a measurable place to judge myself from. It used that external validation to keep me feeding it. It required me to find places, standards, and situations to keep it alive. But in filling my enough-ness tank from within, the extremes no longer served me. They were no longer fuel but now a hindrance to my enough-ness journey.

YOU DECIDE

What we tell ourselves, the "tapes" we play in our heads, have a powerful impact on what we believe about ourselves and about our situation. And while I always knew this to be true, my thoughts on how to achieve healthier tapes were backwards. I believed that once I achieved the clean house, my tape would change to, "I am a good housekeeper." I hoped that once I spent enough time with the kids and engaged with them enough, my tape would change to, "I am a good mom." If I could only hear from others that I was doing the right things and trying hard enough, the tape would change to, "You do enough." I was always waiting for an external situation to determine my internal state. I needed an abundance of proof and evidence to support changing my tape to a different one in hopes I could then believe those things about myself. The reality is, however, that I had to change my tapes first for my beliefs to follow.

There is a big difference between knowing you need to change a tape and deeply believing in that new truth. When I first started, I didn't know that the tapes I was playing in my head were damaging and simply untrue. I truly believed I wasn't doing enough, wasn't a good enough mom, friend and wife, didn't have a clean enough house. I thought the only way to change the feeling was to achieve a behavior that supported the opposite, to have a clean enough house, to be a good enough mom, to do more. Through the process, however, it became clear that those tapes were one of the biggest parts of the problem. If I was ever going to change my situation, I was going to have to change those tapes.

For a long time on my journey, I deliberately chose new actions based on the belief I wanted to own, instead of defaulting to the actions that supported my belief that I was never enough. I started carving out more space for self-care workouts in the morning, but there was still the nagging guilt about the dirty house or spending more time with the kids or getting some work done. I knew the behavior was the right one, but turning it into a deep belief that I felt was the right behavior—that was a different story. I *wanted* the healthier decisions to be my deeply held belief, but they always felt more like an understanding of a truth than something I believed.

I knew the behaviors were healthier and more in line with how I wanted to live my life, so I stayed the course. I continued to choose the actions that represented how I wanted to live my life, even if it took a little longer for the deeply felt beliefs to follow. Eventually, little by little, those actions took root. They became automatic and my new default instead of the decision I had to work so hard to make.

In many ways, my burnout was a blessing. It forced me to look more objectively at what was causing me so much pain and to make changes in my life. But the reality is, if I wouldn't have burned out (though looking back, it was a matter of when, not if), it is likely that I would have gone on for the rest of my life chasing the external validation for enough-ness, living in the stress that need for validation caused, weighed down by the guilt that I allowed those tapes to create.

My hope in sharing all this is that you don't wait for a nervous breakdown to decide to change your tapes. That you too realize you have a choice in what tapes you decide to play. I know it's tempting to want to wait for the belief or situation to change so you can then buy in. But I assure you, that's not how it works. *You* choose the tapes you play. *You* choose how external forces affect you. *You* get to decide the kind of life you want to live and what you buy into. And that starts by deciding what tapes you want to play.

The first step I had to take was recognizing I was playing tapes that were out of whack with a healthy life. The next step was recognizing *when* I was playing the tape. I had to become aware of the guilt, perfectionism, and expectations I was putting on myself without realizing it was a tape instead of a truth. I had accepted them as fact. The tape told me there was a standard of good and I simply wasn't living up to it. In order to change my belief, I had to identify it as an unhealthy tape and as something I could choose to believe or not. Then forcefully reframe what I wanted my new truth to be and choose a different tape.

In the beginning it was a slow process of listening for the tape and consciously shifting the internal belief to an external choice. I had to hear the internal critic. Instead of feeling shamed by it, I had to choose a different path by changing the actual script I told myself.

For example, when my kids asked me to play Candyland and there were dinner dishes in the sink, was I able to sit and play without guilt or distraction? Absolutely not. Not at first, anyway. I would sit on the floor, playing Candyland while thinking the entire time about all the dishes in the sink and feeling terrible that I was thinking about the dishes in the sink. But honestly, at first, that's the best I could do. My only course of action was to change the behavior that I no longer wanted by tapping into the belief I *knew* was the healthier belief even if I didn't wholeheartedly feel like the right decision.

Situation One: Lying in bed before starting the day

Old Script

I should get up. There is so much to do today. I should work out before the kids get up.

But the bed is so cozy. I never get to sleep in. The kids were up so many times last night. I am going to lie here until the kids get up.

But I should really get some work done. And that bathroom really needs to be cleaned. I haven't cleaned the bathroom in two weeks. We are gross. I need to get up and clean.

But I am so tired. I could really use a few extra minutes of sleep.

(Repeat, repeat, repeat until the kids come bounding into the bedroom to start the day)

Result: *I felt exhausted, already behind in the day, frustrated that I neither enjoyed those five minutes in bed, nor got any of the things done that I had been lying there thinking about, guilty for all the things I didn't do.*

Intentional Script Change during the process

I should get up. There is so much to do today. The kitchen needs to be cleaned and I need to work out.

But the bed is so cozy. I never get to sleep in. The kids were up so many times last night. I am going to lay here until the kids get up.

But there's so much work to get done. And I seriously need to work out. (Recognizes tape and makes conscious script change to reinforce the beliefs I want to have)

But recharging your batteries this morning is just what you need. Just lie here and be thankful for the quiet of the morning. (Closes eyes and breathes deeply)

But there's so much to get done today. (Changes script again)

Yes, and you will be better prepared to tackle all that work when your batteries are recharged and fresh. Lie here. Rest. Recharge.

But Good Moms have clean bathrooms.

No. Stop. Enjoy these few minutes. You can tackle the bathroom later. Spend these few minutes quieting your mind and just enjoy the peace. (Actually enjoys a few minutes of peace before the kids come bounding into the bedroom)

Waking up: *I still felt tired, but proud of myself for recognizing the tape and fighting against it. More peaceful because of those five minutes of rest that I actually enjoyed and hopeful that I would be able to continue to recognize and change the tapes sooner next time.*

. . .

Default script now:

Script one: I should get up. But I am tired, and it's been a long, few weeks. I can tell that my body needs the rest. (Rolls over, goes back to sleep)

Script two: I should get up. But I am tired, and it's been a long, few weeks. I'll just lie here for another minute. (Begins to think through all the things that need to be tackled for the day).

Okay, time to get up. If I can't quiet my brain, I might as well get some things done.

In both scenarios I end up feeling happy and proud I was able to listen to what my body and mind needed in the moment and that I didn't let shoulds, guilt, or expectations drive my decision making. More engaged in the day and more at peace with myself.

Situation Two: Walking into my kitchen and opening my junk drawer

Old Script

Oh, man. This thing is such a mess. How does it always get so out of control? Look at this—there is stuff everywhere! You can barely even open it. Good Moms don't let their houses get like this. Good Moms set good examples for their kids with organized drawers and cabinets. They have these things under control and don't let things get this crazy.

Walking around the rest of the day: *Felt ashamed and lazy. Frustrated that I didn't have more organization in my house. Unmotivated. Looked at every single place my house that wasn't perfect with a microscope, judging myself for how much I was failing.*

New Script

Man, this drawer really is a mess. It's hard to even get open. This thing has gotten out of control. You really should do a better job . . .

wait . . . no. Don't do that. You have a TON on your plate right now. This drawer doesn't matter nearly as much as the balancing act you are doing to keep the house clean while spending time with the kids and keeping yourself sane. This drawer doesn't matter.

But while you stand here, what CAN you do to make the drawer more manageable? (Shuffles a few things around).

Wait. Why are there seven grill lighters shoved in this drawer? No wonder this drawer is so hard to open. (Grabs them from the drawer and puts them in the garage) There. That's better.

Walking around the rest of the day: *Feel nothing after I walk away from the drawer. I forget about the drawer all together and go on with my day.*

WHERE'S MY TRANQUILITY RUSH?

Before I knew it, it was again time to head back to the beach for our annual trip. I had spent a lot of the last year working hard on myself and making slow but steady progress. As we pulled in the beach house driveway, I looked forward to the peace that always overcomes me there. I was ready to feel the tranquility wash over me as I watched the sunrise and sunset and listened to the waves crash. The first kid-free morning, I set my alarm and headed out the door for my first sunrise walk on the beach of the year. As the sand slipped through my toes, I waited in anticipation for the giant wave of relief. But it didn't come. I walked a bit longer, sure that I just needed to let myself settle into the morning and I would feel the release of stress that always came. But as I continued down the beach, it didn't arrive.

Over the next few days, I kept waiting for the big vacation moment, when I finally let go and thought to myself, *I want to stay here forever*. But days continued and the feeling never arrived. The beach was lovely and our vacation was fantastic, but I couldn't find a way to tap into that moment.

One morning while walking the beach, contemplating this unsettling experience, it hit me. While I was happy to be at the beach, I didn't feel all that different than I did when I was at home. It was lovely to have the beach as the backdrop for my morning walks, and the pace of our vacation days were certainly slower, but I didn't feel the giant difference between home Lindsey and vacation Lindsey that I always had before. The peace I felt while at the beach on vacation was darn close to the peace I was feeling at home. It was almost shocking. But the reality was there. The progress I was making was palpable. It had been a long road, but there were real changes that were taking place and I knew I was on the right track.

HATE-SANDING

I don't fancy myself a writer. Honestly, I didn't even start out trying to write this book; it just sort of happened. I guess I had always heard the faint whisperings at different times in my life and had even come up with an idea or two along the way, but after a few pages, I struggled to find direction and always gave up. Sharing this journey in book form had never even occurred to me, until one Tuesday morning. It was a morning like any other as I scrambled around trying to get myself ready for the day. I wrapped up my shower, grabbed my towel, and stood in the steamy bathroom, when out of nowhere, *Enough Already*, flashed in my head. In an instant I saw myself back at that brunch with the Wolfpack, felt the pain of crying in the bathroom, saw the piles of toiletries in the middle of my living room, and felt the new peace in my heart all simultaneously. The book arrived in my soul and willed itself to be written.

I worked all day, spent the evening with my family, put the kids to bed, and sat down to write, having no real idea how to write a book, just knowing that it needed to be written. I remember being two weeks into the project and feeling as though I had to be close to a hundred pages, but when I looked down at the page total, I was at eight. Eight! How was that possible? It's possible because writing a book is hard, very hard. And even though I have believed every author that says it's hard to write a book, I really had no idea. Yet here we are. But I kept at it, not knowing what would ever become of it but knowing that my soul needed to write it and that was all that really mattered. Wondering if anyone would ever actually read it but trusting the pull from the universe to share my story.

A few months after I began writing, I decided it was *also* time to update our bathroom and kitchen cabinets. They were original cabinets and were showing every minute of their eighteen years. While the cabinets themselves were solid wood and in good shape, they were dated, the varnish worn off in spots, and overall, in desperate need of a facelift. I had been wanting to update them from the moment we put in an offer on the house, but at the time we had a twenty-month-old and had just welcomed our son into the world three days after moving. Refinishing cabinets would have to wait, as it turns out, four full years.

It had been suggested that I paint the cabinets (by just about every person who saw them because they were pretty terrible). I struggled to find the right color that would stand the test of time. So, I settled on staining them a deep brown instead. Deciding to tackle this massive project was one thing, but committing to it was another. While I knew it needed to be done and I would love the result, taking on this project seemed so daunting. I had thirty-three cabinet and drawer facings to stain, both front and back, as well as the trim along the floor. This project was going to take the kind of drive yet balance I wasn't sure I had yet. But I finally decided it was time and dove in.

I decided to test out my staining ability on the kids' bathroom cabinets because I figured if they turned out terribly, they would be the easiest and cheapest to replace. To my surprise, they were gorgeous, especially compared to how awful they were before. On to the next bathroom and in a week or so, I had two bathrooms looking pretty fantastic. Finally, my attention turned to the oh-so-daunting kitchen cabinets. The first few cabinets weren't terrible, but after a few more, I could feel my motivation beginning to wane. The tiny detail in the cabinets made sanding tedious. The upper cabinets required more getting up and down on the counter than I had the energy for, and each cabinet needed two coats. With overnight drying time between every coat, each cabinet took a few days before it was functional. On top of it all, I was squeezing this project in at the end of already long days. Once the kids headed to bed, I would sand or stain and then cleanup. Long before the halfway point, I was already hating it and totally over the project.

One night I was sanding the cabinets that house our garbage can and recycling bin, sitting nose-to-can with our garbage from the day, cursing the project. I was so annoyed with the work this was requiring. I lamented how tired I was, thinking about how I needed to write instead of stain cabinets, feeling the pull of the couch but also the desire to have this project finished. It had been a few days since I had spent time writing, and I really felt the need to make some more progress on the book. While hate-sanding, I worked to convince myself that after I was done sanding and cleaning up, I would grab my laptop and write for a while. I wasn't thrilled at this idea, but I reminded myself of the things I wanted to accomplish and committed to finding a way to write.

Somewhere deep in my soul, however, the bubbling of self-care started. As I talked myself into pushing through the hate, the whisper-ings of self-care became louder and louder. I could feel the pull to sit on the couch with a cup of hot tea, coloring in the new coloring book I had gotten in the mail two days earlier. I could almost feel the peace and hear the quiet in my soul that sitting there would bring me. But back to sanding I went, determined to make progress on both projects no matter the cost. Then it hit me.

"You are literally writing a book about burnout and how important self-care is. You need to be smarter than this," I scolded myself. But the desire to do was strong.

"Yes, but if you don't push yourself, these things will never get done and there will just be more unfinished projects and plans. You have to work hard to accomplish your goals," I countered my original thought.

The battle continued. "This is the voice you have been working so hard to move past. The one that says you aren't good enough, that you must kill yourself in order to accomplish your goals, that rest is for the weak and lazy. This moment, and so many tiny ones like it, is the moment where you decide what path you want to end up on. There is no due date on your book or your cabinets. Rest, breathe, give yourself the self-care you know you need."

What did I do? Anyone who knows me knows exactly what I did. I finished sanding the cabinets I had been working on, cleaned up the kitchen, grabbed my computer, and started writing. The "must accomplish, must run yourself into the ground" demons won. I had willed myself into doing once again. But as I sat on the couch, staring at my computer, the cursor blinked incessantly at me and the exhaustion weighed heavy. I had nothing left in the tank. I was done. I sat there for another minute and decided it was time to choose a different path. It was time to be wiser than I had been before. I put my computer on the ottoman, grabbed my markers and coloring book from the bedroom, and sat in silence as I drank tea and colored a page full of wildflowers. As a rush of peace fell over me, I instantly knew I had made the right decision.

As I sat and colored for the next twenty minutes, I realized that recently I had not been creating the space in my life I knew I needed. I was in a loop of constant input again. Between writing, house projects, work, the kids, and a host of things going on in our lives, I had again surrounded myself in doing, creating, and distracting. I was moving from project to project, kid to kid, always thinking about what was next instead of being present in what I was doing. It was easy to see how reflexively I had begun picking up my phone first thing in the morning and then again while waiting for my toast and even more when I sat on the couch with the kids watching cartoons. I had slipped back into the numbness and autopilot of life without noticing and away from the connectedness and contentment I had worked so hard to gain. I knew in that moment I needed to once again focus on creating intentional space.

My intentional space wasn't anything life changing; it was just a few small practices that made me feel centered and connected. It was designating 5:30 p.m.–8:00 p.m. as phone-free hours to disconnect from the world and reconnect with my family. Getting to bed a few minutes early instead of a few minutes late each night to wake up feeling more refreshed in the morning. Picking a few nights a week to engage in input-free time after the kids went to bed with a puzzle or coloring. I realized I had been picking the phone up too frequently, falling prey to the doing traps and had lost my connectedness, contentment, and my joy. It was time to create space in my life again, but this time, much more intentionally.

BUMPING BOUNDARIES

One of the most pivotal parts of real change was looking at the boundaries I had created. Before "the moment in the kitchen," I had always been simultaneously in awe of people who had created healthy boundaries for themselves. When I bumped up into one of their boundaries and they gave me a confident but loving, "No, I can't do that," or "No, unfortunately that doesn't work for our schedule," it stung but I would also think, "Dang, good for you! I could never say no like that!" It was hard to imagine being as sure of my boundaries and where I stood within them. My boundaries had always simply consisted of doing what I thought made others happy, trying my best to avoid guilt, and working to feel like I was doing enough.

As I walked through my journey, I thought creating new boundaries, or any boundaries, really would be required. I figured I needed to establish what were reasonable and healthy boundaries and what were simply continued people pleasing and validation seeking behaviors. All the books about growth, owning your space, and stepping into your bad-ass-ness that I had read all talked about how crucial it is to identify your boundaries. So I set out on the path, bound and determined to establish these boundaries "healthy people" had so that I, too, could say no when needed.

But what could these boundaries be? I would think about them on my walks, I would think about them in the car, I would think about them while scrolling through my phone. (I may have even googled "healthy boundaries," but I didn't connect with anything, and it seemed weird to get my boundaries off a Google search.)

With all this work I was doing, surely, I should be able to identify my boundaries with no issue. But the truth was, I couldn't. The harder

I thought about them, the further away any clear answer seemed and the more discouraged I became. But then it occurred to me that I was treating this like I treated most other things in my life: from one extreme to the next. Expecting that after a lifetime of not having any boundaries, I would swing to the other extreme of creating a list of boundaries that I now suddenly believed.

I decided that instead of fighting so hard to identify them, maybe I should be more diligent in watching to see if any boundaries would arrive organically. I was beginning to trust my path and figured that when I needed to find them, I would.

As I started to pay more attention to my life, it became clear just how demanding the pull of my day was. With two early-rising little kids (I can only think of a handful of times in the first four years of parenting that my kids slept past 6:15 a.m. and most often they were up well before 6:00 a.m.), every morning was spent waking up to someone else's schedule and needs, followed by a full day of moving parts: breakfast, drop off, working in a different office, city or state, picking kids up, dinner, cleaning, bedtime, crash. It was hard to think of even five or ten minutes spent doing anything that I needed or wanted to do. It occurred to me how packed my days were, and that perhaps like my closets, I needed a little more space too.

With all the moving parts of life with kids that little, it was obvious that creating space during the day wasn't really an option, so that left me mornings or evenings. Evenings seemed obvious but the truth was, by the end of the day my tank was drained, and I had nothing to left to give after putting the kids to bed. While getting up earlier than my early-rising children didn't sound ideal, I was beginning to see how hard it was to start my day at the call of others. So, I decided to start waking up early enough to get in at least ten minutes of yoga and a quiet moment on the couch to myself. That evening, I set my alarm for 5:30 a.m., hoping and praying that would be early enough to get a few minutes alone before the kids woke up. Any earlier seemed totally unreasonable. I set out a book that I was hoping to get a few minutes to read in the morning and found the eleven-minute yoga video I was planning to do and crawled into bed, excited to take on a new morning routine.

The alarm went off that next morning and I was ready! I got up and tiptoed my way into the living room. The house was so still and quiet. It was peaceful in a way I had never felt before. Sometimes in the evenings, my husband and I would turn the television off and read or play cards. But even that kind of quiet wasn't the same as this. The evening quiet held all the noise and leftover baggage from the day. It was filled with "did you remembers" and "don't forget tos." This morning quiet was different and incredible. It was void of running thoughts and to-do lists. This quiet was light and serene—almost as if it held all the potential for a wonderful day.

I took out my phone and spent the next eleven minutes getting my Downward-Facing Dog on. I felt every stretch and every breath. I was so connected to the moment and the day. I felt alive and full of potential. It also made me realize how unintentionally and unconnected I spent my days living. Sure, I was working toward being more present in the moments with my kids and my husband, but most of the day was still spent moving from one moment, one to-do list item, and one place to the next. This one morning showed me how I wanted to spend more of my days, with intention and connectedness.

After my final cleansing yoga breath and a whisper of "namaste," I headed to the couch where my book was waiting for me. I grabbed *When Less Becomes More: Making Space for Slow, Simple, and Good* by Emily Ley, as it seemed like the perfect read for my new morning routine. Here is where I would love to tell you that I sat there drinking my tea and filling my soul with her magical words. Unfortunately, this is the part of the story where my early-morning riser thwarted my quiet and peaceful morning. No sooner had I sat down than I heard, "MO-O-O-O-M" bellowing from upstairs. With a deep sigh I closed my book and my eyes, drew in a deep breath, focused on the quiet and tranquility of the living room for another twenty seconds, and headed upstairs to start the day.

While the morning didn't go exactly as I had planned, it showed me what a morning could look like. It gave me hope for how my mornings could feel and the peace my days could start with. I was addicted to the idea of early mornings and there was no turning back.

Note: Over the last few years, I have stuck to my early morning routine. Honestly, it's how half of this book got written! The structure has changed, sometimes including writing down three priorities and three things of gratitude, sometimes having longer mornings to myself as my kids eventually started waking up slightly later, and sometimes barely getting yoga in before I am summoned to start the day with the Mom call. But I can tell you for certain, getting myself up early and starting the day with activities that fill my soul has been one of the single most important aspects of my happiness. Starting with intentional, quiet space allows for me to connect to my day, grounds me in my priorities, and gives me the bandwidth to live in my day as opposed to being run by my day.

Over the course of the next six to nine months, I began to settle into my quiet morning foundation. I began to feel the difference in the way I approached the day, my ability to be more connected to my family, my patience during the day, and my focus on the work that needed to get done. I became addicted to getting up early, and when I didn't carve out that space for myself, I could tell the difference in how I approached and connected to the day. My early mornings soon became nonnegotiable. The difference between who I was when I made time for space in the morning and when I didn't was palpable.

BIG STEVE

Life always seems to afford me the opportunity to share my story with others, or maybe as a type A personality, I create places to talk about my journey. But either way, I cannot tell you how often I hear from people who wholeheartedly relate to my journey and share their stories and struggles. It is absolutely one of the coolest parts of stepping into the truth of my story—helping others find the truth in theirs.

One night, while talking to a girlfriend, who in our house is affectionately referred to as "Big Steve" (though she is neither named Steve, nor is she big), she shared with me her struggle of how she wanted her house to look versus the reality of being a stay-at-home mom with two kids under four during a global pandemic. She spoke to how having a cluttered house was stressing her out. But she also knew that ensuring she had a perfectly clean house would leave her cleaning all day, every day, instead of playing with her kids. She spoke of her frustration and how overwhelming it felt.

During our conversation she mentioned her life coach suggested that she let go of her desire for a clean house. Her life coach used the "life is a jar" metaphor. Big Steve should fill her life jar with the big rocks first, as those are the important things in life. Then fill the jar with stones, then pebbles, then sand, and lastly water. The water representing the things and tasks that don't really matter. The life coach suggested Big Steve should consider a clean house as the water. Big Steve said she had been trying for the past few days to let go of wanting a clean house, but so far, it wasn't working. I asked her why having a clean house was important to her. She said when her house was messy, it made her anxious and stressed out and put her on edge with her husband and her kids.

I too understood that anxiety. My stress in wanting a clean house had started off from a place that left me feeling like a failure as a housekeeper and mom. As I continued my journey, I was able to remove that guilt and feeling of failure. Yet even without expectations or judgment, the anxiety from a messy house never really left. I still carried around the desire for a tidy house even after I was able to shed the need for external validation and the labels I had placed on myself about being a Good Mom and good housekeeper.

As it turns out even on my best day, a cluttered house makes me anxious. However, having a house as tidy as I would like isn't always possible when living the full picture of what's important to me. There is a balance. Sure, I *could* spend all day cleaning, but then I would miss out on time with my kids. And spending time with my kids is *really* important to me. I was hearing the same message from Big Steve. So I shared with her the balance I had found over the past few years.

"Maybe there is a balance between having a house as clean as you would like and spending all day cleaning. I have found that when I focus my attention on having two spaces tidy, my bedroom and a clean kitchen, I can deal with the rest of the house being less than perfect. I don't always *love* what the rest of the house looks like, but having those two spaces clean allows for me to feel tranquility in two important places in my home.

"We work to have the kids help tidy up before bed. We have a 'clean-up alarm' that goes off at 6:30 p.m. every night, and the kids know they have to clean the living room and their bedrooms before they can watch a final *Hey Duggee* before bed. You see, when I told them it was time to clean up, it was nothing but fighting, but for some reason setting an alarm on my phone helped them see the activity differently and they actually buy in most of the time.

"I'm not saying it makes any sense; I am just saying that in our family it works! Which helps to make any final cleanup after they go to bed much easier. It also helps them create the habit of having a tidy house at the end of the day. Additionally, it has helped them realize that if they pick up their toys during the day, they have much less to do when the cleanup alarm goes off. And no matter how the day went, walking into a clean bedroom gives me a sense of calm and allows me to more fully decompress. I sleep better and wake up feeling better to start my day."

She was quiet for a minute and then said, "I feel the same way. Having a clean kitchen and a clean bedroom is important to me too. I can see how focusing on those two rooms would help my anxiety but also be a good balance to ensure I am not driving myself and the family crazy trying to keep the house clean." As we wrapped up our conversation, I was reminded how frequently I had previously lived in extremes. But I now saw that perhaps I was finding my way to more of a middle than I had before.

HOT SHOWERS

I like hot showers; I mean *really* hot showers. I am aware that they are neither good for my skin, nor the environment, but fear not, I take very quick showers. A successful shower to me means that upon exiting the shower, the entire bathroom is a giant cloud. I like to stand in the sauna-like room and breath in the thick air as the cloud remains while I get ready. It is *definitely* an extreme.

The morning after my conversation with Big Steve, I didn't have the luxury of enjoying the time in my steamy bathroom and instead opened the door to the bedroom to grab my clothes and get ready for the day. As I reentered the bathroom, I could see all of the steam billowing out across the ceiling and into the bedroom through the doorway where, as it hit the cooler air, my cloud of post-shower happiness was absorbed into the neutral air of the bedroom. I could feel the cool air rush from the bedroom and into the bathroom across my damp legs.

In that moment, I appreciated the way nature always finds a way to create balance for itself. Even when we seem so hell-bent on extremes, the natural order of our world is to find balance. It was a great reminder of how much better I feel when I let go of my tendency for extremes and instead work to find a more balanced approach. For me, neither a spotless house nor a house that is a total disaster is the answer, but instead identifying the things that matter, the spaces that have the biggest impact on my well-being and focusing intentionally on those things. It's not about making a clean house the rocks but not treating it like water either. They are the stones in my jar. They aren't the most important pieces of my life, but they do have an impact on how I enjoy it. I was certainly making progress. I could feel it.

CONNECTING TO THE PEACEFULNESS

In March 2020, the United States joined the rest of the world in social distancing and stay-at-home measures due to COVID-19. Our lives changed overnight, and we were forced to work differently, live differently, and eventually school differently. The routines we had in place and the progress I was making instantly felt threatened. I had just started feeling confident in my healthy habits, which made figuring out how to navigate our "new normal" daunting. The month was a blur as my husband and I both tried to work from home with our two young kids. It tested our patience, our relationship, and our resolve. As it became clear the pandemic wasn't going away anytime soon, we knew we had to find a way to make the best of an overwhelming situation.

My husband worked in hospitality, one of the hardest-hit industries, and a month into the pandemic he was furloughed. While he became the primary caregiving parent, I worked with my business partner to find ways to transition our consulting business to a virtual model. Those first few months were an adjustment for everyone as we acclimated to our new roles and realities. I worked hard to stay committed to early mornings of self-care with yoga and reading because I knew self-care was more important than ever before.

As I created more space and peace in my mornings, I would see the sunrise peeking out over the horizon during my morning yoga and was struck by how incredibly beautiful and peaceful it was. After a few mornings of staring out my front window as the sun rose, I was dying to get out and connect to that peacefulness I always found at the beach on my early morning walks. I felt like I needed it more than ever. I began to wonder if it would be possible to move my early inside mornings, to outside. Perhaps my husband and I could rotate mornings, leaving me in charge of the kids a few days a week to give him space, and I could take the other mornings for a walk. It felt like a big ask (as he was already doing so much of the heavy lifting with the kids), and I immediately began coming up with all of the reasons why I could never ask that of him.

I took a step back and looked objectively at the situation. Almost instantly, I recognized that enough-ness void and guilt flaring up again. Change the script, I told myself. Asking for a few mornings a week to do something to recharge wasn't unreasonable. In fact, it was completely reasonable! It made me happier, more engaged, a better mom and wife, and was what I needed to stay whole. This was clearly an opportunity to stand firmly in my enough-ness and to ask for what I needed. I also figured that he could use a break from the grind of full-time child-rearing and might appreciate a few mornings a week to sleep in or work out.

I worked up the nerve and talked to my husband one evening about rotating mornings of being on kid duty. I proposed that we could alternate mornings: One person would get up with the kids and allow the other person to have free time until 7:30 a.m. He loved the idea and we started a rotating schedule. So, every Tuesday, Thursday, and Saturday morning, I scheduled a long walk on my calendar. And the off days, I would get up to do my morning yoga and reflection before the kids got up. Slowly but surely, I was carving out time and space for myself, so I could more deeply connect with the life I was living.

Over the course of the next few months, I would walk 5.5 miles three times a week around the lake in our neighborhood, leaving the house just slightly before sunrise so that by the time I got to the lake, the sun would be rising just above it. It's where I did my thinking, idea generating, processing, and recharging. I held tightly to the time and it quickly became my favorite part of the day. Monday, Wednesday, and Friday nights, I would crawl into bed and dream about the sunrise and the quiet waiting for me on the other side of the night.

I began to feel the natural shift under my feet as I continued my journey, and I focused on the things that I needed to stay whole and healthy. I felt grounded and at peace with my days. I was filling my enough-ness tank and creating the life I wanted, even during a global pandemic. And while it wasn't easy, it was incredibly fulfilling. It felt like nothing could ever stop me, and I had found the secret to my happiness!

DEVOTED TO SELF-CARE

What I know to be true about life, is that even after you have learned a lesson or grown in some way, there are always follow-up tests. It's as though life is testing your commitment to the lesson learned. A few months later, a big test came for me. As a consultant, trainer, and coach, my work is cyclical and I feel fortunate that my work fluctuates from manageable, to busy, to insane, and back to manageable again. In the beginning of my early morning journey, my company had a manageable schedule; we were busy, but it was a good busy. As I became more firmly rooted in my commitment to early morning wellness, a large amount of new business came my way.

We had a proposal out to coach four to six people in an organization, and we were ecstatic when we were selected by the client. Over the next few days, however, four to six people turned into eleven, then fourteen, then twenty and twenty-five individuals in the organization. While we were extremely grateful for the work, my schedule went from manageable to overwhelming in just a few days as I added twelve of those individual trainees to my calendar.

As I sat staring at a matrix of names, positions, coaching intake forms, and areas for improvement, I felt the weight of the work that was in front of me for the next six months. Grateful doesn't begin to describe the feeling I had for the opportunity to do what I love, but when looking at how I would integrate these additional sessions into my schedule, it began to feel crushing. Coaching requires showing up to every session fully focused, fully present, and fully ready to listen, guide, and suggest. It requires you to be "on" and to be the very best version of yourself.

As I added the coaching sessions to my calendar and the white space on my calendar all but disappeared, my fear of losing my early mornings increased. I worried about not being able to show up like I needed to while simultaneously worrying about burning myself out again. For a moment, it didn't seem possible. I felt destined to fail.

However, not one to back down from a challenge, I began to think about how I could make it work. It was tempting to give up my early mornings to make room for more time to get work done. Because that is usually the case when our schedules get busy. Any self-care we afford ourselves is usually the first thing to go. But I knew that wasn't the right answer. I had been down that path where giving to everyone else first was the priority, and it led me to full burnout more than once. I knew I had it in me to help the people who needed me and to wrangle the schedule I had in front of me, but I also knew that meant I needed to prioritize taking care of myself. I had to reaffirm my commitment to self-care and make it as important as I considered the coaching sessions on my calendar. If I was going to take care of others, I had to first take care of myself.

Within days, my calendar went from breathing room to a "full go" as they say. I was meeting on back-to-back Zoom calls from 8:00 a.m. to 4:00 p.m. nearly every day and getting to know the new people I was coaching, working to put together coaching plans, and coordinating schedules for the next six months. After that, I was working to get my normal work done after the kids went to bed…and I was still drowning in work.

It. Was. Crazy.

It was *so* tempting to skip my morning routine. I told myself there wasn't time for it. I told myself I should just put it on pause until things settled down. But I knew that wasn't the right answer. I knew the right answer was that I needed my morning routine more than ever.

That's the thing. It's tempting when things get busy to let self-care be the first thing to go. It's easy to see everything else as a priority and self-care as the last thing on the list. But I knew I needed to make sure self-care was first on my list. Because if I wasn't in the best mental shape possible, I wouldn't be able to help those who needed me.

It took a few months to settle into the new groove of such an intense coaching schedule. But I made sure to find a way daily to connect to self-care. Some mornings it was yoga, some mornings it was a walk, some mornings it was riding the stationary bike, some mornings it was sit-ups and weights. But my focus was always on intentional and meaningful self-care. Some days it even meant sleeping in because I could tell my body needed rest from the pace I was running. But I always chose it intentionally and with the focus on recharging in whatever capacity I felt was needed the most.

Eventually, the rhythm of coaching fell into a sustainable schedule. Of course, with that many sessions on my calendar, I remained busy, but thanks to the self-care I had prioritized and the natural groove that working with someone over weeks and months finds its way to, I survived that initial crazy season in life and came out better for it on the other side.

Ironically, many of the individuals I was coaching spoke to feeling stressed out, overwhelmed, exhausted, and frustrated by the pace they were running through their lives, especially during the pandemic. To no surprise, self-care became a major topic, and I shared with them the importance of self-care and how it had become a nonnegotiable part of my life. Many of them began to implement the very same routines I recommended from my personal experience. Over the following weeks and months, I would repeatedly hear them say, "Why wasn't I doing this all along? How was I living my life before? How did I survive without prioritizing self-care?" I was grateful to have had the opportunity to share with them a lesson it had taken me so long to learn and to help them realize how life-changing self-care can be.

As I continued coaching, it became clear that focusing on self-care as a necessity rather than a nicety was crucial to my success, but it also became clear that some days it was hard to prioritize. With so many aspects of life needing my attention, the tug at prioritizing things over self-care was tempting. But as I stayed consistent, I noticed my mind creating new lanes I operated from. Self-care started to become a normal part of my day. It was no longer something I had to decide to do, it was simply another routine like brushing my teeth or eating dinner. It was a baseline for the day.

While this time was hectic, it also gave me a great gift. It helped me begin to develop the boundaries I had been searching for. When guilt crept in for not coming up from my office instantly after my last coaching appointment because I instead took ten minutes to decompress from the day to do a yoga video, I reminded myself of the importance of not just being *with* my kids but with being *present* with my kids and that ten minutes for me would actually make me a more engaged mom when I did go upstairs.

Each time I shooed away the guilt and instead chose engagement in my own well-being, I created a tiny internal boundary. I chose the boundary of mental healthiness instead of the free-for-all that had previously been living in my head. Every time I left dishes in the sink and kept the dirty-kitchen guilt monsters at bay, I created a new boundary about how I would allow myself to think. These tiny internal decisions began to create boundaries that allowed me to gain the strength and courage needed to say no to external boundaries. So while I had been looking for the giant external fences to put up to help me feel more confident in the decisions I was making, the reality was that the tiny internal decisions I was making actually created external boundaries for me as well.

I learned that boundary creation wasn't about hard-and-fast rules (though certainly, there are a few boundaries that *are* hard and fast and shouldn't be crossed). I realized that for me, identifying boundaries was about internalizing truths about myself and about others. The first was realizing that I am worthy of having boundaries. I didn't need to please everyone. I am not responsible for the happiness of anyone but myself. Because of the pull of my enough-ness void, I had spent so much of my life trying to take care of others at my own expense in hopes they would fill it for me. My worthiness was directly related to the happiness of others and the sacrifice it required from me. I wore that badge proudly. I had to take that badge off and choose another. Because the truth is, we are all more than simply caretakers of others. I began to realize that it is only when we stand in our own space and say "I matter too" that we can truly begin to find our own happiness and joy. Because we are no longer working to fill our enough-ness void, we are living more fully in the life we have.

I became addicted to standing firmly rooted in knowing I am enough, even when people didn't like me or a decision I made. I recognized I had to create space between what I thought others thought of me and what I thought of myself. I had spent my whole life relying on the validation and opinions of others as my litmus test as to how I felt about myself. But I began to realize that those two things are not connected. One has nothing to do with the other. My enough-ness journey helped me see that, and as I begun to stand firmly in my enough-ness, the realization that this was a foundation of my boundary building became clear.

At first, I would become aware of the moment after it passed. I would look back and say, "That felt like it was past my boundary of what I would want to happen." And I would make a mental note that I should have chosen a different answer or behavior in that situation. And every time a situation occurred again, I became more and more aware of the boundary that existed. Eventually, I was able to identify the boundary in the moment and either choose a different path from the beginning or course correct in the middle of the situation. I had hoped it would be a clear "this is my boundary," path but for me, it was paying more attention to what connected to the whole, joyful part that allowed me to develop my boundaries along the way.

One Friday afternoon at 3:00 p.m., I was wrapping up my last coaching session. It had been a very busy week. My virtual coaching schedule was still crazy, and the week had been draining. As I sat staring at my computer, trying to decide what to do next, I was tempted both to work longer because I had so much to do and to shut my laptop and walk away because I was so mentally exhausted. As I sat thinking about which pull to lean toward, I realized neither of those options seemed like the right one.

I knew if I kept working just because there was more to be done, I would be distracted, tired, and going through the motions. However, shutting down my laptop and walking away made me worry that I would bring work thoughts with me and not fully engage with my family. In the past, I would have chosen family and raced up the stairs to apologize for working late and taken the kids, leaving no space to be mentally ready to engage with them. I would have simply walked through the rest of the evening on autopilot until we got them to bed.

But now I knew there had to be a better answer for everyone involved.

I decided to spend thirty minutes working out on our exercise bike in the basement. I grabbed a notebook and some water and hopped on the bike. I had a launch for an End of the Year Challenge for my DreamSMALL program a few days from then, and I needed to think through how to make it meaningful and impactful for the participants who had signed up. I started pedaling and instantly knew I had made the right decision. As I pedaled, my mind began to clear and ideas began to flow. The more I pedaled, the more I began to sweat, more the stress from the week washed away, and more space for creativity opened. After the bike, I did some quick weights and sit-ups and headed upstairs to welcome the weekend and reengage with my family.

It was Take-Out Friday, a favorite tradition of ours that began when the pandemic started. After a full week of home-school learning and working, cooking three meals a day, and finding the fortieth game of the day to play, who had the energy to cook and clean up dinner on Friday night? Not anyone in this house, that's for sure. It was always cause for celebration and we played the afternoon away. It's in these incredibly simple acts, in sometimes incredibly short bursts of time, that I realize the real progress that I've made.

It's not about hours away for self-care or girls' weekends in the woods, although that does sound lovely. It's about the time spent doing things that I need and want to do to keep myself balanced—actually caring for myself without the heavy weight of "doing" guilt that previously ran through my head on a constant loop. It's about the example I now intentionally set for my children about the importance of living life more fully, enjoying the life we work to create, and knowing how to care enough for myself so I can genuinely enjoy caring for others. It's become the enjoyment I get from working out and the even bigger enjoyment I get from engaging with my kids afterward.

In that moment, I would see the progress I was making. It felt I had spent years willing a coal train up the side of a steep mountain and it was now on the other side of the top of the hill. All that weight that had made it so hard to get up the hill was now distributing the same force down the hill. I was picking up speed and my momentum was growing by the day.

COSMIC BALANCE

As we packed the car the night before our early morning departure to the beach, I was giddy, not only for a week of walks on the beach, but even more so for what I was sure would be another year of breakthrough moments. Because of the pandemic, we had shifted our vacation, and this year our trip fell over my birthday. I was jazzed. I thought spending my birthday with my toes in the sand and morning walks on the beach was just what my soul needed. My sunrise walks around the lake had become my addiction and I was ready to spend my mornings wrapped in an ocean sunrise.

We had always been lucky enough to have fantastic weather on our vacations. It's not often that we had a rainy day, and I couldn't think of a time where we even had more than one day of rain. This year, however, it became clear that life had other plans. It rained all week. And not just a quick beach thunderstorm in the afternoon. There was a hurricane farther south in the Atlantic Ocean that didn't affect us directly but left most of the week with thick dark clouds and rain that blanketed the sky. Early in the week, I was able to sneak out for a walk, but with the gray clouds hanging low, there wasn't much sunrise to see.

The time spent with family was wonderful and the food was delicious, but my soul yearned for those morning walks and that time and space to myself. I was working hard to keep my frustrations with the weather in check, but a few days in, I lost it on my husband. I don't even remember what I was being snippy and obnoxious about. I couldn't keep it together any longer.

Between rain showers, I grabbed my flip-flops and headed to the beach for a walk. I needed to clear my head and find a way to get myself together. Forty-five minutes later I walked back into the house in a better mood. While I certainly hadn't found my way back to zen, I was closer to functional, which was going to have to be good enough for the time being. The next morning was my early morning to myself because my husband and I switch off mornings even on vacation. That meant it was time for a walk. I went to bed hoping for a sunny morning weather miracle but woke up only to find a sky full of clouds again. I silently grumbled about the unfairness of missing another sunrise but headed out the door toward the beach.

As I walked, I started playing old mental tapes in my head. I struggled with a "this is unfair," "why can't I ever get a break," and "life is so hard right now," mental temper tantrum. I had to work hard in that moment to remind myself that lessons come in ways that make us grow and that clearly, there was something I needed to learn from this experience. I had been reminding myself of that lesson all week, but my frustration at the situation was growing deeper every day. I wanted to hear the lesson, wanted to grow, so the sun would come out and I could get what I wanted—a thought that I now recognize as completely counter to growth. Because if growth is truly happening at a deep level, we no longer need the thing we thought we needed before to make us happy.

As I walked, I came to the giant pier I had stood below two years before. The one with the most amazing orange sunrise that served as the wallpaper on my phone since that day. Now here I was, under the same pier, wanting to update that photo, but instead, gray skies and fog ruled the day. My heart continued to sink and rage at the unfairness. I kept walking, battling the annoyance that laid within my soul.

I had been asking the universe all week for clarity. To help me learn the lesson it was trying to teach me with this obnoxious rain, but I hadn't found it, hadn't heard it, and I was even more annoyed by that. I continued to walk as the frustration rolled through my head, "Other people have beautiful weeks at the beach. I have a friend who had *two* beautiful weeks at the beach this year, and I have a friend who lives *at* the beach. I get up early, I work hard to make myself a better person, I am writing a book to help other people for goodness' sake. Haven't I earned those sunrises I need in order to keep me happy and feeling good?"

There it was. The lesson. Previously, I was using tiny bottles of shampoo to fill my enough-ness void, and now I was using morning walks and sunrises to find my inner peace. I was continuing to use external things to drive my internal state of being. Over the weeks prior, I had many conversations with my coaching clients that focused on the theme of, "You can't allow external factors to impact your internal state." During a global pandemic, there is so much you can't control. While I knew that to be true and whole-heartedly believed it, it became clear to me that I again wasn't 100% living that myself. Sure, I had picked healthier external factors to influence my internal state, but I was still relying on other things to control my mental state of being.

I hit two miles and turned around. Soon I reached the pier again and stood under it, watching the waves crash and staring at the gray skies. This time I could feel my frustration turning to calm and under-standing. As I continued to walk, I kept thinking about the pier two years before and the pier this year. As I listened to the sand crunch under my feet, I realized that the previous years at the beach, my take-away had been to do a better job of slowing down the tornado I was living in, to make myself more of a priority, and to take more control over my mental and physical health, which I had done and done well.

This year, it became clear I needed to find a way to create peace and tranquility within myself and not rely on outside circumstances to experience it. I would continue setting healthy boundaries so I could make the space for my mental and physical well-being, but I would need to learn to let go of the control and my need for external situa-tions to create it. I needed to find a way to create that peace within myself.

Control what you can, let go of the rest, create your own internal peace regardless. Find balance in your journey.

Balance became the word that resonated. Happiness without depen-dence on external factors. I told the universe that was the lesson I was hearing and asked for a sign I was on the right track.

A few more thoughts shuffled around as I continued my walk back to the beach house. As I put on my flip-flops and headed up the boardwalk, a sense of awareness rushed over me. It felt like I had my next path to walk, my next lesson to learn. I knew this was going to be a very big challenge. But I also knew this was a lesson the universe was going to teach me one way or another, so I might as well face the lesson now and work my way through it. Better to pay attention to the rainy day at the beach birthday lesson than to experience whatever loud and truly painful way life had in store to teach me next. Grateful to have heard the beginnings of the lesson, I headed up the stairs and into the house to start the day.

As this was one of the few opportunities to get outside during the week, as soon as I got home, we packed up our bags and headed to the beach. A few hours later, we were on the beach with some extended family who were vacationing at the same time in a beach house nearby. As we sat on the beach together, my husband's aunt jumped from her chair and said, "Oh! Lindsey! I forgot that I have something for you for your birthday!" And she grabbed a present from her beach bag. As I opened the small white box, I saw a beautiful bracelet. I was thrilled!

As I flipped over the card to read the descriptor of the emblem, I smiled to myself. "Cosmic Balance." I smiled to myself knowing that the universe always answers when you ask. And it had delivered in a big way. It was clear. Balance was my next challenge.

YOU ARE A GOOD MOM

A hot and sunny Wednesday in August 2020 was the first day of virtual kindergarten for my daughter during the pandemic. Clearly, it wasn't the first day of kindergarten we had imagined, but the upside was that I cried a lot less than I normally would have because she would be attending school in her bedroom every day. As my husband was now filling the role of primary caregiver, he was in charge of virtual learning but would also have my son during the day to do "Daddy school." We knew it was going to be a lot to tackle. With two kids who were still very little and needed a lot of caregiving, the split of places and needs was going to be intense, especially at first. I had taken the morning off work to help everyone get settled into our new life. After a great breakfast, we started to get the kids ready for school.

The night before I had laid out five dresses for my daughter's first day of school, all adorable and ones that I loved on her. When I asked her to pick which one she wanted to wear on the first day, she ran upstairs to her dresser, bypassing all my first-day-of-school dress options, and grabbed her favorite short-sleeved, gray, cotton dinosaur dress. She ran down the stairs, proudly waving her dinosaur dress, yelling, "It's my favorite! And it's so comfortable!" How can a mom argue with that?

She excitedly put on her dress as the clock neared 8:45 a.m. (when virtual school started), and we headed to the front porch for pictures celebrating her first day of kindergarten and my son's first day of Daddy school. While my husband and daughter went upstairs to her room to get her settled in for the day, I played with my son in the living room. We knew it was going to be a lot of work to navigate helping our daughter as she learned how to use her computer for live interaction with a teacher and students while managing and entertaining a four-year-old. But I knew my husband was up for the challenge. My son and I played for an hour, but with my aggressive coaching schedule, around 10:00 a.m., I headed to my home office, leaving my husband to juggle both kids for the remainder of the day.

That evening we all reconvened at the dining room table for dinner. We discussed the day and I asked my daughter all kinds of questions about her teacher and how her first day was. She had loved seeing all the kids on the screen but was quickly shocked to learn she would be going back to virtual school the next day. She wasn't thrilled at the idea, but we continued to reassure her we would all get through this together. We survived the first day unscathed but slightly more nervous about what the school year had in store.

After putting the kids to bed that night, I grabbed my planner—a habit I work hard to stick with—and sat down to fine-tune my plan for the following day. I looked at my schedule and saw that it was my morning without the kids, which meant I had a walk around the lake in our neighborhood coming up. I instantly felt torn. I knew day two of virtual kindergarten would look a lot like day one, and I could feel the guilt rising. My husband was going to have his hands full getting my daughter settled in and helping her mute, unmute, know when to come back from breaks, and stay focused in a way she had never been asked to before, all while managing our younger four-year-old who would most certainly want to spend his day outside playing in the dirt in our backyard.

I had two very clear thought patterns. One was a desire to stay home and help my family navigate the second day of school because, after all, it was a *lot* for one person to handle. The other was knowing that I needed the walk to ensure I could show up for my family and my clients in the best possible way. I was still knee-deep in coaching and it was taxing. I could feel the deep fatigue at the end of every day, and I knew that taking time to recharge daily was crucial to keep going at the pace I was. Both seemed equally big and important to be there for.

> *Enough-ness note:* The fact that I felt the guilt to stay home,
> while still giving credence for the need for self-care shows just
> how far along I was during this part of my journey. In any time
> before then, I would never have even considered prioritizing
> self-care. It wouldn't have even been in my realm of possibili-
> ties. I would have defaulted to "Good Moms take care of their
> families first, no matter the personal cost." I can see now that
> this moment was one of those subtle wins as I recognized that
> my own mental health was just as important as everyone else's.
> It was a change that over the course of time was becoming my
> new default: "Good Moms take care of their families, while
> also taking care of themselves."

But as I thought about which was the right decision, there was something deeper pulling at me. It was the bigger picture about where these paths would take me. As a person who had struggled for so long to put up reasonable boundaries to keep myself as a priority, this felt like a huge test of those boundaries. I kept asking myself, which do I choose? Do I make things easier for my family by staying home to help with my son while my husband and daughter navigate this new school situation for a second day? Or do I prioritize what I need to ensure my mental health stays in check with the heavy load I am carrying?

It felt like a nearly impossible decision, but as I went through the course of the evening, I reminded myself this would be the new normal for us for the foreseeable future. They were going to have to figure this out without me as I spent my days working in my office. I reminded myself that I had taken the morning off, I had been there for my family, I had spent the evening prepping everyone for success the following day. I had taken care of them and now it was time to ensure that I was also prioritizing my well-being. I needed to keep myself mentally healthy and strong for the long haul ahead of us. I knew the only right answer was to go for my walk in the morning, even if it felt hard. So I quieted the old guilt tapes, pulled deep from the hard work I was putting into my new decisions, and set out my walking clothes and shoes for the next morning.

As summer turned to fall and the sun started rising later in the morning, I was fortunate to be able to move my schedule around to accommodate the change. Most of my coaching clients were in California and I live on the East Coast, which left my mornings flexible. On Tuesdays and Thursdays, I worked from 5:30 a.m. to 7:30 a.m. and then scheduled 8:00 a.m. to 10:00 a.m. for a walk and a shower. Online school for my daughter started at 8:45 a.m. So, after breakfast with the kids, I headed to the bedroom to get myself ready for my walk while my husband got our daughter ready for school. I could feel the guilt growing, and I was working hard to choose the tape I knew to be real and healthy, but the old tapes of guilt and shame started bubbling up.

"Maybe you should just stay home one more day to help. You have this huge block of time on your calendar that you could help get her settled and then play with your son. Going for a walk seems so selfish when you are just getting into this routine. You could always pick it back up next week."

Guilt was making incredibly logical and rational arguments in its attempt to keep me home. But I knew the importance of this walk wasn't just about today. It was about heading down the slippery slope of always putting others before myself. Always making the needs of others more important than my own needs. Always looking for outside situations to prove that I was a good mom, good partner, and good human. And if I didn't go that morning, it would become even harder to do it next time. My family was going to have to figure out how to do it without me at some point.

I stood in my bedroom and changed the tape to a better one. "You are a Good Mom. You have a lot on your plate. They need you to be your best self. Today is as good as any for them to start getting use to the new routine."

As I walked out of the bedroom, I could hear my husband helping my daughter get ready for the day and saw my son playing in the living room with his toy cars. This was the moment when I put all this work to the test. I walked upstairs, kissed my husband and daughter, and told them to have an awesome day. I headed downstairs, zoomed a Hot Wheels car down the track that was sprawled across our living room and kissed my son as I headed out the door.

I was expecting a giant wave of guilt to hit. To feel the weight of Bad Mom arrive and to fight through it. But instead, as I stepped out of the door, I felt proud of myself.

It was not the choice I would have made a few short years ago. It wasn't even a choice I would have *considered* a few years ago. But here I was, making myself as much of a priority as everything else in my life. As I walked, I did feel the twinge of guilt arrive because I knew for certain we had a long road ahead of us, but I didn't feel the gut-crushing blow of guilt that had previously accompanied putting myself first. I knew I had made the right decision. I was continuing to solidify the path that I wanted to be on instead of defaulting to the path I had always operated from. It was time to move past the tapes and enjoy the path ahead.

AND A LONG, COLD NIGHT IT WAS

We have a group of friends who get together every year to camp on a large plot of land near where one of the couples got married. We all meet the second Saturday in June to celebrate their anniversary and spend an evening playing volleyball, sitting around a campfire singing songs, eating s'mores, laughing way too hard, staying up way too late, and eventually finding our way back to our tents for the night. My husband and I have been taking this camping trip for nine years, and it's one of my favorite annual traditions. The year of COVID-19, however, we pushed the evening back from June to September and maintained extra social distancing precautions to ensure we were safe.

We live in Maryland, which means in September, it could still be 95 degrees Fahrenheit on any given day. That year, however, was unseasonably cold. The temperature was 64 as a high during the day and 38 degrees at night. We usually make this a night away and my in-laws take the kids, but because we were being very cautious during the pandemic, having them watch the kids wasn't an option. So this particular year, we and a few other quarantining families all brought their kids for a more family friendly version.

As we were camping in colder weather, I bought some thermal sleeping bags that had great reviews, packed up the tents and food, and headed to our annual camping trip. I was as prepared as I could be. It was a fantastic evening; the kids had a blast and we spent many hours laughing in socially distanced family pods and retelling stories from years gone by. The kids rode bikes and ran around, mostly just thrilled to be with other kids after being separated for so long. We ended the night with a campfire, glow sticks, and s'mores. It was picture-perfect and just what we all needed after a few long months of quarantine and pandemic.

Then we all headed to bed for the night. As we walked away from the warm and cozy campfire, we quickly discovered how cold the evening really was. We walked swiftly to the tent, hoping those sleeping bags lived up to their promise. But as we crawled into our sleeping bags, it was instantly clear their promise of warmth had been a lie. It was freezing in the tent and in our sleeping bags. As we closed our eyes, it became obvious it would be a long, cold night.

And a long, cold night it was. About an hour after entering the tent, our daughter woke up freezing, and even after putting her in every clothing item we brought for her, she was still freezing. She then climbed on the air mattress with my husband and me, shifting both of us to the edges, leaving us dangling from the sides for the rest of the night. On the other hand, my son who always runs warm, pulled the sleeping bag up over his head and slept warmly and peacefully through the night. Between the cold and having three people on the queen-sized air mattress, it was 4:00 a.m. before I fell asleep. Both kids woke up at 7:00 a.m. still cold but ready to play again. We all woke up, headed to the car, turned on the heat for a few minutes to warm ourselves up, and off they went to play again while my husband and I started packing up the tent and toys.

We pulled into our driveway at 11:00 a.m. and swiftly dropped the load of camping items in our living room as the kids headed to the couch. We were all pretty tired, but as it was Sunday and we had been gone all day Saturday, there was a lot to be done for the upcoming week. Earlier in the week, my husband had asked for two hours to watch the Chelsea soccer game from 11:30 a.m. to 1:30 p.m. that day. After unloading the car, he headed down to watch the game. The kids asked to watch a movie on the couch, which I happily obliged. I was tired, but I knew if I sat down, even for a minute, exhaustion would take over and the day would be a wash. If I was going to get anything done, I had to start right at that moment. It was time to get down to the business of unpacking, cleaning, and preparing for the week.

I spent the next hour unpacking the suitcases, starting the laundry, and putting away food. I then tackled all the things that needed to be done for the week, I changed our sheets and purged food from the fridge from the past week while I put together a grocery list for the coming week. The following hour found me continuing to get our house back into shape.

As I walked into my son's bedroom to put away some toys, I remembered the cloth baskets I had bought to organize the top of his closet. So, I headed back downstairs to grab the bins and back up to his room to get organizing. Once that was complete, I started putting away our camping equipment, only to I realize I needed a place for our new sleeping bags. I had an extra bin in the basement, so I grabbed it and began organizing our camping things to ensure easier packing for our next trip. After that, it was time to get lunch ready for the kids. As I stood at the kitchen sink prepping lunch, I realized I needed to make bread for the week.

As I prepped the yeast, flour, salt, and water, I heard the kids laughing at the movie and felt the peace that always washes over me when I make bread. I thought about what a lovely day it was. I was exhausted, potentially even beyond exhausted, but it also felt good to be making so much progress in the house and doing so many things to get myself organized.

Then it hit me, another wave of how things had drastically changed but also hadn't changed that much at all. Four years earlier, the day probably would have gone much the same way it had that day. No matter how exhausted I would have been, I would have plowed through the house, taking on more projects than were reasonable and probably even necessary in that moment. But that's how I am wired, take charge, push through, make things happen, no excuses.

But this time, there were two very big differences. Differences that reminded me how far I had come and how grateful I was to have changed my life.

The first: In years past, I would have been doing all the cleaning, organizing, and prepping in hopes that my family would notice how hard I was working, realize how tough I was, and praise me for being so amazing. I would spend the day working my butt off waiting for recognition and validation. The "Good Moms have clean and organized houses" tape would be playing in my head. I would be moving from room to room, doing my best but beating myself up about all the things still undone. I would have been lamenting that even though we had agreed in advance to the downtime to watch his favorite football club play, my husband wasn't helping me with the list of chores *I* decided were extremely important in that very minute.

I would have been in full anger cleaning and organizing mode, waiting and hoping desperately for praise and validation the whole time, even though no amount of thank you would have ever really made me feel validated. I would have walked around frustrated and feeling unappreciated for the rest of the day. I would have gotten the house clean and organized, but I would have spent the day miserable, angry, and feeling resentful.

However, this time felt different. I was cleaning, unpacking, baking, and organizing for a very different reason. There was no Good Mom tape running through my head. There was no frustration at my husband. I wasn't waiting to be validated and patted on the back. I was accomplishing all these things while feeling calm, peaceful, happy, and dare I say, proud. Don't forget tired, as I was still definitely tired. I was working hard. I was potentially superhuman that morning for being able to tackle all the things I had on very little sleep. But mostly, I was proud of myself! I was setting myself up for a successful, productive, and enjoyable week. As I stood at the counter kneading bread, I realized what a true badass I really was! But I didn't need to hear it from someone else; I finally knew it for myself.

The second key change, and this is an important one: self-care. After lunch, I needed to give the kids a bath. As my daughter climbed into the tub, I sat down on the floor. She was thrilled to be in the water and immediately started playing. All of three minutes into her bath, it hit me. The wave of exhaustion I had been trying to avoid for the last few hours. I tried to fight it, but it latched on and took me down. She kept asking me to play tea party, but it was all I had in me to keep my eyes open. As luck would have it, my husband's soccer game ended, and he came up the stairs to see what he could do.

In years past, I would have clung tightly to my doing badge, my "I need to prove to everyone how tough I am" and my "I need people to see me working hard so you can tell me how great I am" ego. I would have told him I was fine. I would have fought through, waited for that validation I had worked so hard all morning for, and been super annoyed the whole time. Instead, I looked up at him and said, "The kids are fed. The house is in decent shape. You're in charge. I need a nap." He looked at me and said, "Great! I've got this. You've got to be exhausted. Go take a nap." So I did. I walked into my bedroom, closed the curtains, crawled into my freshly made bed, and closed my eyes. It was the most glorious nap of my life. I was exhausted, but I was proud of myself, both for all I had accomplished, but even more so for the progress I clearly had made.

I woke up two hours later and willed myself out of bed. I was still tired but knew if I slept much longer, I wouldn't sleep that night. Upon walking out of the bedroom, my son looked at me and said, "Let's go outside and play!" This wasn't exactly what I had in mind for the remainder of the afternoon, but his big brown eyes pleaded with me for some mom and son time, so on went my shoes and out the door we headed. It was a beautiful day, and we spent the next hour or so playing dinosaurs in our front yard and watering the flowers. It's not often that you see in real time the progress you are making nor how far you have come. But in some unexpected moments, you can see the past and the present simultaneously and realize just how lucky you are to have walked the path you did, because you are so much better for it.

HOW, WHAT, AND WHY

Those who know me well know that I had a not-so-secret desire to turn forty. Ever since my early thirties, I was not-so-patiently waiting to hit the Big 4-0. While most people run from turning forty, I was dying to get there. At first, I couldn't identify why it seemed like such a magical number and why I was so excited to get there, but as I hit my mid-thirties, it became clear. Reaching forty seemed like a turning point, a mile marker, and solid ground upon which to stand. It felt like once you were forty, you would have your life together, you would have the solid foundation of who you are underneath you, you would be confident and settled in yourself. I was hopeful that once I turned forty, magically, the insecurities and frustrations would disappear, and I would be replaced by the woman I wanted to be. I was so attached to and vocal about this desire, I had a friend throw me a fortieth birthday party when I turned thirty- eight. Like I said, I *really* wanted to be forty.

As my thirty-ninth birthday drew nearer, everyone began to ask me if I was excited to be thirty-nine as that would put me only a year away from my fortieth. I was surprised when I realized I wasn't actually all that attached to the idea anymore. While I was looking forward to my birthday, forty somehow didn't have the same draw as it had years earlier. It wasn't that I didn't want to turn forty, it was more a feeling of being content being thirty-nine.

A few weeks before my birthday, I watched a Simon Sinek video on Instagram. He said, "Is what you're doing and why you're doing it consistent? Because only when your why, how, and what are in balance do we know who you are."[7] These words, like so many others I've talked about in this book, hit me deeply. I never thought about my why, my purpose, my what (what I do every day), and my how (how specifically I accomplish those things) being in or out of balance. But when I took a step back, I realized that for most of my life, I lived out of the very balance he was talking about. My why and what were cloudy at best, which made my how scattered, stressed out, and tired.

But the last few years, I'd been working hard to clarify my why and what and changing the how I did daily. When I heard Simon Sinek's words, it hit me that all the work I had been putting in was working. My external life didn't always feel in balance. I mean, there was a global pandemic, virtual homeschooling, and four humans almost always trapped in a house. But thanks to the work I had been putting in over the past few years and the daily effort I was making, I had found that balance internally. The life I wanted to live was much closer than it had ever been.

Instead of spending my mornings lying in bed, fighting with myself about what I should be doing, I was waking my family up at 6:00 a.m. to go sunrise chasing. This is a favorite activity of mine where we jump in the car in our pajamas and drive to our favorite spot to watch the sunrise while eating granola bars. I was staying connected to the things that made me feel whole and happy. I was shedding unrealistic and unhealthy expectations, taking much better care of myself mentally and physically, and being better able to care for those who needed me. I was living in harmony with my why, what, and how and it felt damn good.

I now realized turning forty wouldn't have given me all the things I had hoped it would. Reaching forty wasn't the promised land to suddenly feeling settled and solid—the past few years' worth of hard work was…which made celebrating thirty-nine even better.

FRANTIC LIGHTHOUSES

One afternoon I found a profound quote by Anne Lamott that perfectly reflected the shift in life I had made: "Light- houses don't go running all over an island looking for boats to save; they just stand there shining."[8] Most of my life I had been the lighthouse running across the island looking for boats to save. I was running everywhere, trying to save everyone and everything while desperately hoping to get noticed. However, as I walked my enough-ness path, it became clear I had settled into the role of the stationary lighthouse. Confidently standing in my own space, brightly shining my light, hoping to help those around me.

You see, in theory, the two types of lighthouses aren't that different from each other. The only real differences are *why* and *how* they shine their light.

I didn't know I was the frantic lighthouse, though I definitely was. I thought I was the thoughtful and supportive lighthouse always running around finding a place to be needed. But now I can see the value of the lighthouse that stands firmly in its soil and helps those it can, by being constant, impactful, and at peace with its place in the world.

SPROUTS

My Grandma, or as I called her my whole life, Bobbie, was my best friend. Her name was Helen, and it's a long story as to how we got to Bobbie, but that's the only thing I ever called her. I would spend weeks at a time with her during the summer at a little house up in northern Michigan that we called the Farm. She came to every dance recital, called me her Angel, and we each thought the sun rose with the other. Even in college, I would come home to spend the whole weekend at her house without telling another soul I was home.

She lived a life worthy of a book. She had Frank Sinatra sing to her in a bar in Hamtramck, Michigan, and kept a spare set of clothes in the trunk of her car so that after a night out with her girlfriends, she could change before going to work the next morning. These are only a few sharable stories of her awesomeness! She lived and loved passionately.

She was never afraid to ask for what she wanted. She believed when money came to you, you should save half and spend the other half on whatever your heart desired. She gave religiously to those in need, and she never backed down from a good political battle. She was loving and stubborn, beautiful and funny, and a take-charge but soft-spoken lady. She was fantastic. In 2007, she passed away, and not a day goes by that I don't still miss her. After her funeral, we gave most of the flower arrangements to the nursing home she had been living in, but there was a plant in a basket that I took for myself.

There are a lot of things that I can figure out and find a way to make work, but a green thumb has never been a skill of mine. I have killed just about every plant I have ever owned. I have killed plants people have sworn I couldn't kill. I have killed cactus and succulents, ferns and bushes. I mean, I am *really* good at killing plants…except that plant from Bobbie's funeral. As of 2020, that plant had lived in six different houses and in nearly as many rooms in each of those houses. Plus, consistent watering wasn't exactly my thing. I tried to remind myself weekly to water it, but it was more often that I remembered a few days after I noticed the leaves beginning to droop. How that plant is still alive nearly thirteen years later, I have no idea. I can't help but think the plant must have so much of Bobbie's spirit in it to be alive after all these years with me as caregiver. It's as lovingly stubborn as she was, which makes me love it that much more.

This past year, I realized it needed a transplant. It had been far too long since I had done anything to it. The dirt was brown instead of black and sinking in around the plant, and it had aggressively outgrown its container. It clearly needed a face-lift. A few weeks earlier, I had fallen in love with some pots that I had recently seen and asked for them for my birthday. With my new pots in hand, I headed out to the garage to transplant Bobbie's plant. Before long, the single plant was now divided into three pots, and my heart was full. I watered them and placed them lovingly in my living room.

Every day I walked into the living room and saw my new pots and the plants that I loved so much. It made me feel accomplished in caring for them, and I simply adored the new pots. The following weekend as I was watering the plants, I leaned in and noticed five new leaves shooting up. I was thrilled! I walked to the next pot to water, and there were four more brand-new stalks of leaves! Then I walked over to the original plant and found half a dozen leaves! They were the brightest green I had ever seen and incredibly adorable.

That evening, I sat on the couch half-watching TV and half-thinking about those new leaves sprouting. The original plant had been in the container for the past six months with no new growth, perhaps even a year. Steadily and diligently holding strong but not growing anything new. It was surviving, though given my black thumb of plant death, even survival was incredible. It made me think about my journey over the past few years. I too had been stuck, just trying to survive. Living my life, while trying very hard to make it through every day, but ultimately, more surviving my life than living it.

But over the course of just one week, I had three plants that were now sprouting new life. That were greener than they had ever been and added even more joy around my house than the one standing alone. All it took was some new dirt and giving each part of the plant the space and care it needed. Within a single week, it was more alive than ever. That is exactly how my journey felt. With more space to breathe, some fresh perspective, and lots of self-care, I too was beginning to sprout new life. I too was more vibrant than I had ever been. I too was adding joy in lots of new places. I had always loved that plant, but somehow in that moment, it made me feel more connected to my Bobbie than ever before.

THE FIRST 30,000

A few months and about 30,000 words into writing this book, I saw that the Nonfiction Book School with the great Stacy Ennis was being offered. I knew of her through my professional network, and she was highly regarded as the best of the best when it came to writing. She has authored and coauthored several great books, one of which I use in my professional career for leadership training. I began to wonder if this might be an opportunity worth pursuing. With all the time and energy I was putting into the book, it felt like this could only help me make the book the best it could be. I reached out to Stacy and instantly fell in love with her. It was easy to see why she was so respected in our industry. I knew she was the person to guide me through the rest of my book-writing journey.

Then I looked at the price tag. While a completely reasonable price for her expertise and the value she shared with all of us, investing in myself was a new concept. I hadn't historically spent much money on myself. I don't care for designer items, preferring TJ Maxx over fancy stores, and usually ask for new sheets, kitchen items, or new yoga pants for my birthday and Christmas. I just don't connect with expensive things and definitely don't buy them for myself.

A few months previously I had fallen in love with a $65 necklace I saw in a Facebook ad. I looked at it for months and just couldn't get over how fantastic I thought it was. But $65 felt like a lot of money to frivolously spend on something for myself, so I continued to scroll past. One day, as I was nearing the end of cabinet staining, the project that I still haven't fully mentally recovered from, I thought, *I should ask for this as a present for all the hard work I put in on the cabinets. I saved our family over $2,000 by staining them myself, and if we would have replaced them, it could have been over $20,000, so $65 on a necklace seems fair.*

It was a big ask for me. And while perhaps it was something I could have just purchased myself, asking for it as a present felt so much more impactful on my journey. It was the opportunity to say, I would like to be recognized for my hard work. My husband was thrilled that I was finally asking for something and happily bought me the necklace and had the kids give it to me as a thank-you. It felt like a huge victory, and I still wear it with pride to remind myself that I am worthy of vocalizing what I need and want. And because it was from my family made it that much more special.

But that was $65. Book school was more than $65 and it felt like a *very* big ask. Not only of our family budget during a global pandemic, but also to invest in myself in a book that I didn't even intend to write. So, I began to ask the universe for a sign. I had sent the first 30,000 words to a few friends and was getting encouragement back that they loved the book and that they related. But I was looking for a big, giant sign from the universe. I was looking for a "this book is so great, there is no way you can't sign up for book school" message so I could feel justified in it. I asked and waited, asked and waited. Nothing, no sign.

I had the book in the hands of a dear friend and family member (also named Lindsay Weigle, though an-ay, not an-ey like me), who actually helped inspire me to write and wonderfully, thoughtfully, and talentedly, edited my book along the way. It had been over a week. I was anxiously awaiting her feedback. I needed to make a decision on Book School by Friday at midnight, and I spent all day on Friday looking for a sign from the universe that I was worth investing this much money in.

Which is exactly when it hit me. I was writing a book about *being enough*, and I was asking the universe for a sign that I *was enough* to invest in. I mean, if you can't feel like you are enough to invest in while writing a book about being enough, then you should probably just stop writing immediately. I realized this decision wasn't about book school; it was another opportunity to decide if I really, truly felt like I was enough and if my story was worth telling. Did I believe that something my soul was calling me to do was enough reason to bring this book to life, or was I still more focused on external validation to fill my enough-ness void?

The decision became clear. I had to sign up for book school and invest in myself to make this passion project the very best it could be. And even if my mom was the only person who ever read it, the investment in myself was worth it. Because validation doesn't come from the outside; it never has. Validation comes from the deep knowing that you are doing things and living your life in a way that makes you feel more *you*—alive, happy, free, and joyous. That afternoon, I signed up for book school.

As is usually the case, once I had figured out the lesson and decided what direction I needed to head, the universe answered my call. The very next morning, I got an email from Lindsay saying she loved the book and was so grateful for the stories and lessons I shared in it. I swelled with pride in hearing these words. It certainly felt great to hear such validation from someone I respected so much. But there was another layer of pride I felt as well. I was proud I had chosen to invest in myself without external validation, because though it felt good to know someone else related to it and found value in it, I also had found that value in it for myself.

As I knew would be the case, book school not only helped me become a better writer and find the parts of my story I needed to share, but also forced me to continue to confront things on my enough-ness journey that both made this book better and rooted me more deeply in who I am and how I live my very best life every day. Investing in myself has now become a practice that I can't live without. It continues to shape me and forces me to grow as I continue my journey.

WARNING SIGNALS

It's not often you get the opportunity to look back at a nervous break-down—a full burnout, total life-altering experience, call it what you will—with true gratitude and knowledge that you were being cared for. I fully believe the universe is smarter than I am, and it's always giving me the things I need, even when it doesn't always look like it. But looking at my life over the past few years, it continues to be clear to me that the universe *was* taking care of me, even when it all felt so overwhelming.

Under normal circumstances in my professional life, our trainings and coaching are conducted in person, which means we can only do one training per day mixed with a few coaching calls. Our process changed with the pandemic. Moving to a virtual format meant that there were no more 3:30 a.m. wake-ups to get to DC by 8:00 a.m.

because my training was now on the computer in my basement office. There were fewer logistical limitations between client appointments because Zoom meetings allowed us to swap quickly from client to client, which in many ways was a blessing.

It meant I got more snuggle time on the couch with my kids in the morning and I saw them throughout the day as I came up from my office to get something to drink or make lunch. I wasn't fighting traffic after a training session only to get home having missed dinner with my family. I was able to prioritize family walks after dinner through the woods in our neighborhood. Plus, I wasn't on airplanes or in hotel rooms for days at a time during training programs.

There were a hundred reasons that working virtually was a huge advantage. The downside, however, is that you can jam-pack your schedule to the brim because there is no reason not to. As coaching continued into the fall and we continued to book more business, my schedule went from crazy to bursting at the seams. There were weeks when people would request to move a scheduled coaching session because of a conflict, and I genuinely didn't have a single slot to offer them in my week. I was up at 5:15 a.m. working out, writing this book, working all day, spending evenings with my family, and working into the night to stay caught up or at least functional.

At first, it was invigorating. I love the work that I do and helping so many people felt incredible. The privilege of being able to help others on their journey while they were struggling during unprecedented times like a pandemic was never lost on me. Of course, it was busy, but it was also energizing.

However, as the fall wore on, so did the grind I was under. Most weeks I would have upwards of 20 individual coaching sessions and virtual trainings, and more than a few weeks, I was pushing 27 or 28 coaching sessions and trainings in a single week. It was back-to-back-to-back-to-back Zoom calls, jumping from one client situation, need, lesson, or struggle to the next. All needing me to arrive refreshed, focused, present, and with ideas, questions, and suggestions to help them navigate all the things taking place in their world. I was also in the middle of a behavior change/goal achievement end-of-the-year challenge for my DreamSMALL program that was requiring inspiring, informative, and supportive emails three times a week to my participants. My plate was full, very full. It was an amazing time, but it was also grueling, and it began to take its toll.

I was working hard to keep my spirits up, staying healthy and engaging in activities, like my exercising and morning quiet time. However, I could feel my energy waning, I could feel the tug of the exhaustion, I sensed that I needed to be careful.

In the beginning, my early mornings were lifesaving. Even when I didn't set an alarm and told myself to sleep in, I found I was naturally up at 5:22 a.m. I relished the time to myself and the quiet reinvigorated me. However, as the grind wore on, that began to change. I began to feel the drag as I tried to get myself out of bed. Yoga in the morning felt more like a punishment than a recharge. I found myself hitting snooze when the alarm went off and not waking up again until 6:15 a.m. Thankfully, six years into parenting, my kids started waking up a little later.

I was soul tired at the end of every day. I needed rest of mind and body to keep up with the pace I was running at. If I am honest, I *was* tempted to double down and ignore the desire for rest and stay focused on doing as I had always done. My job was to inspire others, to show them they could tackle the things in front of them, to show them they could create the life they wanted, and that consistency and willpower were magical forces to keep you moving in the right direction.

Coaching and my DreamSMALL program had momentum, and I didn't want to let anyone down. Doing seemed like a must to show them they could do it too. But I knew the reality. I needed to let go of the expectations of the world and to care for myself. I knew hitting pause was truly what I needed. I needed to listen to my soul.

After that realization, I recalibrated what success during this time looked like. I let go of the expectations I was putting on myself and worked to find a way to keep myself mentally healthy during such an overwhelming time. I needed to be very clear on my priorities and stay very focused on what truly mattered. It was clear that meeting my work expectations was necessary and being able to engage with my clients the way they needed me had to be a top priority.

I also needed to decide how to prioritize my family. What did success as a mom and wife look like at this time? I knew being present was of utmost importance. I wasn't getting the amount of time I wanted with them, so ensuring the time I did have was connected, without distraction, and meaningful was most important. Next was my house. I needed to determine a new baseline as to what I expected my house to look like. What was clean enough? What was a priority? How much time and energy did I have to give to it? The final question addressed self-care. How much time and energy could I commit to ensuring I stayed on the right side of good?

This time, the stops signs were brighter than before, the warning sirens louder. Sure, I still felt the tug to keep up the momentum to prove I could handle it all and inspire others to do the same, but this time, I was smarter. I knew there was a top to my capacity tank. I knew there was no willing myself through this situation. If I continued on the path I was headed, I would end up in the very same place I had been before.

This time, my priority was to ensure I was happy, healthy, and taking care of the things that I wanted and needed in my days. I prioritized wellness, even in a circumstance that felt overwhelming and exhausting. I proactively kept myself out of burnout that would absolutely have come, and I ensured I enjoyed the life I was leading, no matter how busy. So, this time I chose differently. I stopped my morning workouts, I crawled into bed at 8:30 p.m., I read books at night instead of watching TV, and I didn't send quite as many texts to my friends. I went into a deep state of self-care to ensure I could maintain my well-being and balance.

This is not to say it came easily. I'm not going to pretend that many days as I woke up at 6:30 a.m., knowing I hadn't worked out at all that week and feeling every bit of it in my waistline, that I didn't hear the little voice in my head yelling, "WIMP! A tougher person could handle all of this *and* get a workout in." But I was able to put that voice in its proper place. I could fully recognize it was not of one in rightness, but of one out of habit, shame, and residuals from my enough-ness void. It was a script that no longer worked for me or held any weight, and I was able to recognize it as a tape I no longer chose to believe.

IN A FLASH

I often think about the similarities of my personal growth with how growth happens with kids. Seeing them every day, you don't often notice them getting bigger. Inevitably, you'll be with someone you haven't seen in a while, and they will say, "Man! The kids have gotten so big!" You tilt your head a little and look more objectively. "Sure, yes, I guess they have gotten a little bigger," willing yourself to see the changes.

But then one day, you're standing in the kitchen cooking dinner, and they come running up behind you. You turn around and the light hits them just the right way, or they ask a question they never would have asked before, or they come up higher on the counter than they used to and BANG! It's like a flash. It's all you can see. They are so much bigger!

That is how my transformation hit me. One night after putting the kids to bed, I stood in the space between my living room couch and my bedroom. One direction would lead me to doing more in the day and the other to indulging in an early bedtime. I grabbed my computer and crawled into bed to write for a bit and within minutes knew it was time to sleep. I had given the day all I had and knew that going to bed early would put me in the best position to maintain the pace I was running. I leaned over, put the laptop on my dresser, and turned off the light. As I sank into the pillow, I felt a wave of contentment wash over me. It was about more than engaging in the self-care that I needed; it was in doing it without guilt, without question, and with total peace in my heart.

In that moment, the growth I had made was palpable—I was able to make a better decision, to recognize the critical voice not only didn't serve me, but was no longer one I valued or agreed with. To choose health over guilt, to be able to freely switch between being a productivity rock star at work to an engaged mom, a person with a semi-clean house, a good friend, and a daughter who still called her parents not because she *should*, but because she wanted to. Because I was making a difference in the lives in those around me in a way that added happiness in my heart, instead of crushing anxiety and ineptness.

I could feel the internal shift as clearly as I could see the growth of each child when we measure them in the doorway on their birthday. It might not be something the rest of the world saw, but that didn't matter, because I didn't need that external validation the way I had needed it before. I closed my eyes and slept better than I had in years.

BANANAS

Every year since I was a little girl, for Christmas I have bought my dad a daily calendar for his office. You know the ones: a daily hockey trivia fact since we are hockey fans, facts for left-handers like him, or weird presidential trivia that resonates with him. Last year, in the hustle and bustle of the holiday season, I accidentally bought him two daily calendars—which he doesn't need now because he is now retired, but hey, traditions are traditions! So, my house ended up keeping the extra, "Did You Know" calendar. It's filled with all sorts of odd facts and useless trivia. I decided we might as well use it and put it on our bathroom counter. As strange as that seemed at first, I grew incredibly fond of it and have continued this tradition. While brushing my teeth one morning and changing from one day to the next, I saw the day's odd fact was about bananas. While we know bananas as a curved fruit, when they start growing, they grow straight down because of gravity. However, as they continue to grow, they curve upwards towards the sun, ultimately giving them their curved shape.

Now, there are a *lot* of random pieces of trivia I read about every day from this calendar, but this one made me think. I had never even considered wondering why bananas are curved. I just took it at face value that they are. But the more I thought about it throughout the day, the more it resonated with me how incredibly cool it is that bananas grow toward the light against gravity. It also struck me how my journey mirrored that of the growth of a banana. For so long I was growing with gravity—the pull of social norms, the pull of the life I was living, the pull of the experiences and pressures I allowed in my life. That was, until I decided to grow into the light.

I decided to choose a different path than that of the way I was growing and the pull of my original gravity to instead grow toward the sun, the happy, the peaceful. I never thought to stop and consider if my truth was reality or if there was another path, but once I began growing into the light, there was no turning back. And much like there is an undeniable shape to the way a banana grows, there is an undeniable arc to the growth I have taken. Both are real, both are visible, and both make for an interesting truth about growth.

PUT HER DOWN

A senior monk and a junior monk were traveling together. At one point, they came to a river with a strong current. As the monks were preparing to cross the river, they saw a very young and beautiful woman also attempting to cross. The young woman asked if they could help her cross to the other side.

The two monks glanced at one another because they had taken vows not to touch a woman.

Then, without a word, the older monk picked up the woman, carried her across the river, placed her gently on the other side, and carried on his journey.

The younger monk couldn't believe what had just happened. After rejoining his companion, he was speechless, and an hour passed without a word between them.

Two more hours passed, then three, finally the younger monk could [not] contain himself any longer, and blurted out, "As monks, we are not permitted [to touch] a woman, how could you then carry that woman on your shoulders?"

The older monk looked at him and replied, "Brother, I set her down on the other side of the river, why are you still carrying her?"[9]

As I continue my journey, perhaps the biggest shock is my ability to clearly see how much I was carrying around that I didn't need to. To be aware of how I used to speak to myself and weigh myself down, creating so many obstacles to happiness and wholeness. Putting heavy expectations on myself that I didn't need to. Letting so much of the outside world determine my inner state. When none of that needed to be my reality.

The decision to choose a different story, decide my own path, and cultivate my own worthiness has been the single most important thing I have done in my life to date. It has led to health and happiness, better conversations, and deeper joy. It's a foundation that has made me stronger and able to carry more, as well as discerning when to put down what doesn't need to be carried.

The thing that has stuck with me through all of this is how frantic life felt before my burnout. There was always something to be done, to be cleaned or to be made more perfect. I remember running out the door on more than one occasion, grabbing my computer bag, lunch bag, and purse as I threw myself in the car. More times than I care to admit, I would put my seatbelt on and grab the nail polish I kept in the car. I would hurriedly swipe each nail, attempting to cover up the tips that had chipped, hoping desperately they would dry before I got to my client's office for training. While this was certainly a resourceful use of time, it felt so frantic and reinforced the feeling that I was always just barely keeping my life together.

Here's the thing: There is a reality to needing to have nicely painted or naturally manicured nails in the line of work I am in. As a facilitator, speaker, and trainer, individuals are most assuredly making judgments about my competence and credibility based on how I present myself, nails included. Ensuring I arrive "polished" from head to toe to nails is something I consider a part of my job.

However, it was the *way* I did it that was the problem. It was the story I told myself about being the woman painting her nails in the car before leaving the house. It was the leaning into the tornado of life and the guilt that always accompanied it. *A more together person would have made time for this last night and wouldn't be painting her nails in the car at 6:15 a.m.*, I would berate myself. And there I would sit with wet nails, driving to a training, full of shame, while making promises to myself to be better next time.

During my busy coaching and training season, I was being interviewed on a podcast that would be recorded with video. I was nervous, both on being interviewed and especially about what to wear. After getting ready and settling into my desk to review the questions we would be covering, I looked at my nails and realized they needed some help. As I sat painting them only minutes before the podcast began, I laughed to myself at the idea that some things never change. Thankfully, I wasn't driving anywhere, but I hoped I wouldn't need to write anything down, because my hands would be out of commission for the next 20 minutes as I was daring enough to attempt two coats only minutes before the podcast.

As I sat there, laughing at my last-minute polish, it occurred to me how free of self-judgment I felt. It was certainly important to look put together, but I didn't feel the franticness and guilt that had always accompanied this activity in the past. I could recognize the importance of polished nails but also knew that they didn't determine who I was, what I could accomplish, or how put together I actually was. They are a societal standard that I choose to buy into without allowing it to make me feel frenzied or internalizing my worthiness based upon it.

Without realizing it, I had found that natural balance and a natural boundary. I set a boundary that prioritizes the external standard for having well-kept nails, which for me means polished, while not internalizing what it says about me. It's these small moments when I realize how far I have come. It's in noticing the absence of guilt when I wonder when the tide shifted, and I began to find my own ground underneath me. So much of the first part of my journey consisted of big, life-altering moments that are forever burned in my brain as I uncovered new truths about myself and worked to change the tapes. The journey to change those truths have been many tiny nail-polish moments strung together.

NERVOUS BREAKDOWN GRATITUDE?

One Thursday, I was talking to my mom on the phone about how much I had on my plate. We were still adjusting to virtual school and virtual work, we had a house that felt very lived-in every day, and we were working through all the emotions that were coming from the abrupt life change we were all experiencing. I could hear the pace of my speech increase as I began to get myself in a tizzy about all we had going on. She could hear my stress, acknowledged all that I had on my plate, and asked how I was handling it all—in the most loving way that only moms can.

I sighed deeply and prepared to throw myself on the martyr sword about all we were carrying. But in that moment, I paused and thought more deeply about the question. I had called my mom while I was on a walk around the lake in our neighborhood one beautiful summer morning. It was still early and the lake was quiet. I had yet to see a single soul. I had initially called my mom to check in on her, but the conversation had ended up being about how we were managing everything. As I looked around and listened to the stillness, I realized that even in the middle of the turmoil and unknowns and "busier than evers," I was out for a walk. I had prioritized my mental health. I was taking time for myself without an ounce of guilt or worry if that was what a Good Mom would do with her morning. I knew in my soul I was doing the right thing for everyone by taking some time for myself.

As I walked, I said to her, "You know what? I know there isn't ever really a great time to have a nervous breakdown, but I am *so* grateful that it happened when it did. It had seemed like the worst timing ever with all that I had going, which to be fair, was definitely part of what led to the burnout. But here's the thing. If I wouldn't have had burnout when I did, there is no *way* I would be surviving this pandemic as well as we are. Sure, we have a lot going on, but overall, we are happy and healthy and enjoying the time we are spending together as a family. I am clear on what needs to be done and what my priorities are.

"If I wouldn't have figured this out a few years ago, I have no doubt this pandemic would have pushed me over the edge. My ability to prioritize my mental wellness, my enough-ness, self-care, and imperfection is what has made this pandemic survivable. It is what has allowed me to see the good in situations that are so hard. It's given me gratitude for the opportunity to re-craft our life in a way that works better for us."

In a way, the pandemic feels a lot like my life did during my journey. For many years, we as a family were juggling work schedules, extracurricular activities, holidays, friends, family, and expectations. It often felt like we were going through the motions of the week just trying to get to the weekend. Then the pandemic hit suddenly, a lot like my nervous breakdown hit, and without much warning to prepare. It also put our lives into a full stop. It changed the way we looked at everything and made us live differently than we ever had before.

But what is crazy is that much like all the good that has come since the day of my breakdown, so much good in our lives came from the pandemic. It forced us to re-evaluate how we live. It gave us the opportunity to reprioritize how we spend our money, how we spend our time, what we focus on, and what we want the rest of our lives to look like.

I am aware that not everyone is as fortunate. I know there are a lot of big, hard things that have come from this pandemic for nearly every individual. For us, we were forced to shift and regroup in a way I don't think we ever would have in a "normal" situation. I can't help but hope this, too, was a blessing in disguise. That the time where our external lives were brought to a full stop and forced us to consider if we were living the life we wanted or living the life we had is ultimately the universe taking care of us one more time.

I am forever grateful to have made these changes over the past few years to prepare me for what was truly coming into our world. As always, the biggest blessings usually look like the biggest disasters first. I always knew I was lucky to have hit a breaking point that required me to reconstruct my life in a more sustainable and enjoyable way, but man, am I ever grateful it happened when it did.

GUILT AS A SUPERPOWER

I've talked extensively about guilt in this book, and for good reason. My guilt was all-consuming and overwhelming. I remember feeling incredibly guilty most days for showering. The tape playing in my head was, "A Better Mom would have gotten up earlier and taken a shower before her kids were up, so she could be playing with them now instead of showering and missing out on this time with them." There wasn't an activity or moment that I couldn't find a way to feel guilty about. It's almost as if I wore feeling guilty as a badge that I *was* a Good Mom.

Obviously, my journey has taken me down a different path, and I now see how detrimental, unnecessary, and exhausting guilt can be when it's your default emotion. When I was being crushed by the weight of the guilt I carried around, I always thought the goal was to get rid of it. To find a way to erase the pain guilt causes. However, as I have continued my journey, I now realize that guilt is my superpower! Hear me out.

I told stories earlier about my crazy schedule that led me to prioritize taking care of myself so I could avoid burnout while still being able to care for others. And it worked! I passed the life test. However, as the year wore on and the holidays approached, my schedule stayed consistently busy. I was also working to finish this book and get it published. I had a *lot* I was trying to juggle, and I could tell I was *doing* my way to the tipping point of burnout. I kept telling myself that I needed to be careful, that I needed to work harder to take care of myself. But day by day, week by week, my self-care began to wane in order to make room for editing, buying and making Christmas presents, and condensing coaching sessions into smaller periods of time because of the holidays. I was exhausted and concerned.

The good news is that I wasn't motivated to complete the items on my to-do list because I felt like I should or that's what a Good Mom would do. I didn't feel the weight of the enough-ness void as I sat for hours meticulously making homemade presents for friends and family. I did all these things because I wanted to—both because they were things that needed to get done for work or they made me happy to be able to create and give to family and friends.

The bad news, however, is that regardless of the reason, the pace was too much. I had too much on my plate. I feared I was nearing burnout quickly. I was moving from thing to thing, email to email, and kid to kid again. One night as I crawled into bed utterly exhausted, I felt it hit. I knew my engagement and patience level with the kids was off and the guilt came crashing around me. I laid there for a moment in the familiar heaviness of mom guilt. I started to change the tape to one about not feeling guilty for doing what needed to be done during this busy time when I stopped myself in my own tracks. The objective truth was I *was* too busy. I *wasn't* spending the amount of time with the kids that I wanted. I *was* nearing burnout at an alarming rate. I knew this because I was once again getting warning calls from my friends and family, which is always a great indicator about how much I was doing and the pace at which I was doing it.

Now that I had worked to remove the unnecessary and harmful guilt, I had cleared a path to use guilt as a warning signal. To use it as an indicator when things *were* out of balance, when I *was* living unsustainably and nearing a disastrous end. It turned out guilt wasn't something to eliminate entirely. When in its proper place, guilt actually works as a superpower to help me see when I am living out of balance.

In that moment, I realized that no matter how busy my schedule, I was still in charge of how I lived my life and how I spent my days. I decided how many things I put on my to- do list. I decided how I spend my out-of-work hours and how much I let the busyness of my days impact the time I spent with my kids…and I decided how close I let myself get to burnout again. I now know the dangers of what burnout looks like in my life, yet here I was, dancing way too close to the fire. It was time to get it in check. It was time to adjust what was on my plate, to ask for help where I could, eliminate what I could, and manage the rest better than I was.

I wish I could say that I magically cleared my schedule and my stress plummeted. But honestly, it took me longer than I anticipated to truly reduce my pace and my stress. But that's the reality of change.

Sometimes we nail it and sometimes we simply do better than we did last time. I consider my experience a victory because I didn't hit full burnout. I was able to see the end coming and worked diligently to turn around, starting by pumping the brakes a bit.

The truth is I am lucky. That recent situation could have ended very differently because I was very close to my limit. It made me realize that the problem with the capacity tanks we all have is that you never truly know where the top is. It's hard to be sure of just how much we can handle until it's too late. My goal now is to keep myself far enough below my breaking point that I don't need to worry about it. This experience showed me how quickly life can escalate, and it's my job to keep myself far enough below the top limit that I never again know where the top is. As it turns out, guilt can be the superpower that saves me from myself and my deep-rooted tendencies.

THOSE MONSTERS

Somewhere in the middle of my journey, I found a podcast by Oprah and Eckart Tolle called *A New Earth*. It's a ten-part series that walks through Tolle's book, of the same name. There were many insightful and perspective-altering conversations the two had during the many hours of this podcast. However, one that has stuck with me over many years is Eckart's perspective on stress. He explains that stress is our reaction to wanting something to be different than the reality that is in front of us. When we spend our time living in the stress of wanting reality to be different than it is, it blocks us from being able to make the changes we desire. It sounds counterintuitive at first, but it's actual genius.

It is only when we accept the current reality, that in the moment, the thing in front of us is how it is. We really *do* have that many things on our plate, the person *is* making a choice we don't like, our child *is* driving us crazy that day. We then are clearheaded enough, not distracted and frantic because of the stress, to make a good decision about how to fix, change, or move away from the situation. It's not saying we are fine with the situation. Instead, we accept the fact that the situation is the reality in that moment, and instead of internalizing the stress from that reality, we accept and move into changing what we do not like about that situation.

Eckart's words have continued to ring in my ears through the past few years. They help me take a step back when I am frustrated. They help me gain my composure when I am feeling overwhelmed. They remind me I have more control over a situation when I remain level-headed instead of allowing myself to get caught up in the emotion of the moment. They help me stay centered when I feel like I'm being blown around in the tornado of life. Because the reality is there are times when I still feel overwhelmed, when I still feel like there is too much on my plate, when my cabinets still feel too cluttered, and my house still feels too messy.

The difference between then and now is that I am not weighed down by connecting any of those things to my self-worth or my enough-ness. I am not fighting monsters that keep me away from being able to deal with the challenges life throws at me. I have a more direct path to making things better, faster. I am not creating more drama and frustration because of those deep-rooted desires to prove my worthiness and enough-ness.

It is rare that I hear those monsters any longer. Those tapes that I played so often and so methodically for years have either been thrown away or are buried deep in a box in the basement, because they don't often find their way to the light any longer. They live in my memory of a time that helped me arrive into the person I am today: still flawed, still working hard, still challenging myself to step bravely into who I want to be but now with freedom from the guilt, self-judgment, and need for external validation. As I continue through my enough-ness journey, my focus has transitioned from working to fill my enough-ness void to where I look forward into the person I continue to become, to the life I continue to create, to confidence in my journey and the lessons I want to teach my children. It's transitioned from a life of reaction and self-doubt to a life of ownership, direction, and enough-ness.

Much like the lesson I learned in my late twenties—the biggest blessings usually look like the biggest disasters first— my enough-ness journey has been no exception. It's a journey that has transformed the way I look at life and at myself. It's changed the way I live, and as I continue to share my experience with others, it's one that I am finding is all too familiar to many. My goal of this book has never been about assuming my story was anyone else's but rather to share my journey and hope that it helps others on their own. That somewhere amid the strife and struggle, the tears and frustrations, the hope and wisdom, someone else may relate and it may help make their journey a little easier.

WHAT YOU WON'T FIND HERE

Through this book, I've shared a lot with you as to my experiences, my tapes, my habits and my enough-ness journey. As we near the end of this part of my journey, it's worth a moment to stop and talk about what this book doesn't talk much about, and that's what you should do if you are on a similar path. In books similar to this that I have read, there tends to be a lot of advice given: Ten steps to reducing your stress, five sure fire ways to happiness, etc. What you won't find here are three, five or 10 steps to enough-ness. That's because I don't believe I have the answers as to how YOU find enough-ness or happiness. I think that happiness doesn't come in a few simple steps or another to-do list item. I *do* hope, however, that my story has shared insights that have made you think differently about your path, made you question the tapes you play, given you a different perspective on self-care, but mostly, and made you consider if you are living the life you want or simply managing the life you have. At the end of this book, there are a list of questions that I hope you review and take a few minutes to answer for yourself.

What I know about my path is that nothing I figured out was earth-shattering or rocket science. It's mostly all things that I had heard before, but it wasn't until I had no other choice but to listen and learn that I truly began to understand the lessons they were all trying to teach me. My wish is that this book serves as a stepping-stone on your path.

Not a prescriptive, here is what I think you should take away from this book or here is how you should live your life, but a story shared designed to engage in your life in a way that adds value and joy. Enough-ness was the cornerstone of a number of behaviors in my life that stole the joy out of my days, that may not be the same for you. Everyone has different battles and challenges they have to confront.

NOT FULL CIRCLE

In all good books, as the story ends, the author finds a way to circle back to the beginning. They tie together the pieces from where they started, and they create a neat little bow around the story. As I worked to finish this book, I kept trying to circle my story back to the doctor's office where this all began to unfold. But try as I may, I simply couldn't find a way. And for a while, it bothered me. It felt like the story deserved that bow; it should circle back around to give the reader a sense of closure.

But as I continued to write and think, it occurred to me there was no way I could circle the story back. Because since that day in April, after so many Aprils of going to the doctor for the same stress-related symptoms, I hadn't been to the doctor for any issues at all, other than my annual wellness visit. I haven't hit a wall without knowing why. Anytime I have been insanely busy, I have been taking good enough care of myself through the process, so I come out feeling better on the other side.

That's when it hit me. I can't tie it back to the doctor's office because this story isn't a circle, it's a journey. There is no neat little bow, because the journey is a path forward into the future, not a circle back to where I have been. I am deeply and ultimately changed from the person I was that day to who I am now. And I am grateful for every tear, every step through the mud, every friend and family member along the way, every opportunity for growth, and every minute of joy that I have come out with on the other side.

As I share versions of the draft with others, it's been amazing to hear how many people share incredibly similar experiences, tapes, and pitfalls. If you have related to the journey in this book, know that you are not alone. There are thousands of people out there just like you. Their story may look a little different, but their experience feels just as real.

So, in the last few words of this book, the real question becomes, what are you going to do moving forward on your journey? Maybe you have been making realizations along the way and have begun to change your tapes. Maybe it has opened your eyes to a part of your journey that you didn't have a way to articulate before. Maybe this has made you question the guilt you place on yourself or the perfection you strive for. Maybe you now feel the faint whisperings of an enough-ness void that demands your attention and energy. Maybe you see places that you are settling for "good enough" instead of creating something fantastic. Whatever has connected with you, my hope is that you realize you are not alone in your experience and find a way to share your journey with someone who can be an advocate along the way.

Perhaps share this book with them. Or maybe just share a story from the book that you relate to and see if it connects with them as well. The biggest blessing this book has provided me to date is a platform to talk about this topic in a way I have never been able to before. To acknowledge the struggle, to talk about what is weighing us down, to help individuals recognize the ability we all have to choose different tapes, and to start living lives that bring us more joy and happiness.

My wish for you is that you are brave enough to continue your journey, that you walk the path that leads you to the realization that You. Are. Enough. Just as you are. We all are.

QUESTIONS

Questions to consider as you continue your enough-ness journey. (These also make great book club questions!)

1. Have you read other nonfiction self-help books like this one? If so, how does this one compare in terms of being applicable to your life?
2. The author finds a lot of meaning through TV shows, books, and podcasts. Can you relate to her experiences? If so, which ones?
3. What section of the book resonated with you the most and why?
4. What is the first moment in your adult life you realized you might be experiencing burnout? Explain.
5. The author shares that overachievement was what she thought she needed to do to be enough. Do you feel that same way? Why or why not?
6. The author shares how guilt eventually became her superpower to indicate when she was out of balance. What is yours?
7. What actions or thought patterns in your life do you think lead you to times of imbalance?
8. When in life have you found yourself settling for "good enough" instead of crafting something marvelous?

9. What actions, thought patterns and activities do you use to avoid dealing with how you are feeling?
10. The author thought she was doing self-care with manicures and brunches with friends when really self-care is much more than that. What activities give you a false sense of self-care versus activities that truly make you feel rejuvenated?
11. What insights have you taken from the book that you can apply to your life? How do you plan to get started?
12. How do you plan to ensure you notice the subtle, positive changes you are making?

I would love to hear your experience and how you related to the book. If this book has connected with you, email me at lweigle@bluewater-advisory.com.

To learn more about the DreamSMALL program—our online, self-paced behavior change program—email benslow@bluewateradvisory.com.

To learn more about the coaching and training we do at Bluewater Advisory, visit www.bluewateradvisory.com.

Follow *Enough Already* and share your journey on Facebook and Instagram.

NOTES

ENOUGH ALREADY

1. Valorie Burton, *It's About Time: The Art of Choosing the Meaningful over the Urgent* (Nashville, TN: Thomas Nelson, 2019).
2. Tenneva Jordan, GoodReads, accessed May 23, 2019, https://www.- goodreads.-com/quotes/502972-a-mother-is-a-person-who-seeing- there-are-only.
3. Malcolm Gladwell, "McDonald's Broke My Heart," *Revisionist History*, season 2, episode 9, August 9, 2017, http://revisionisthistory.com/episodes/19-mcdonalds-broke-my-heart.
4. *Dr. Seuss' The Lorax*, directed by Kyle Balda and Chris Renaud (Los Angeles, CA: Universal Studios, 2012), DVD.
5. Oprah Winfrey and Jon Kabat-Zinn, "Jon Kabat-Zinn: Mindfulness 101," in *Oprah's SuperSoul Conversations*, podcast, September 23, 2018, https://omny.fm/shows/oprah-s-supersoul-conversations/jon-kabat-zinn-mindfulness-101.
6. Joshua Becker, *The More of Less: Finding the Life You Want under Everything You Own*, read by the author (Old Saybrook, CT: Tantor Audio, 2016).
7. Simon Sinek, "Can Your Personal and Professional WHY Be Differ- ent?," Insta-gram, September 1, 2020, https://www.instagram.com/p/CElzl6rJcxD/.
8. Anne Lamott, *Bird by Bird: Some Instructions on Writing and Life* (Palatine, IL: Anchor, 1995).
9. "Two Monks and a Woman—A Zen Lesson," *Stories of Kindness from around the World*, KindSpring, traditional story posted by ahihalau, June 20, 2014, https://www.kindspring.org/story/view.php?sid=63753.

ACKNOWLEDGMENTS

This book would not be possible without the love and support from my husband (Gabe), my kids, Mark and Mom, Dad and Judi, Lindsay Weigle, Courtney, my Wolfpack (Jenn, Tiffany, and Amy), Mark, Julianna, Jenn, Rachel, Lauren, and Shannon.

Thank you all for your support, your inspiration, your encouragement, your patience, and your love throughout this process. You have helped make this book a reality, and I could not be more grateful for each one of you.

These truly talented professionals were incredible resources helping me every step of the way, and I am incredibly grateful.

Editing:
Kim Foster
www.kimfostereditor.com

Photography:
Sarah Rachel Photography
www.sarahrachelphotography.com

Marketing:
Kristen Elworthy
www.sevenhillscommunications.com

Promotion:
Joanna Harrison
Founder and CEO of Tiger Rose Communications
Joanna@tigerrosellc.com

Cover layout and design:
Rene Folsom
&
Stacey Smekofske
Editor and Author Coach
EditsByStacey.com

Nonfiction Book School:
Stacy Ennis, best-selling author, speaker,
and founder of Nonfiction Book School
www.stacyennis.com

Proofreading:
Stephanie Hendrixson

**Note: I am especially proud that they are all small, women- owned businesses.

ABOUT LINDSEY WEIGLE

Certified Professional Behavioral Analyst & Certified Professional Values Analyst

Lindsey is one of Bluewater Advisory's two Partners. Bluewater is considered an elite firm in the Talent Management business and adds significant value to organizations throughout the United States in three primary areas:

1. Leadership & Organizational Development
2. Succession Planning with comprehensive talent, operational and organizational alignment
3. Recruitment and selection strategy.

In addition to serving as project lead on various client engagements, Lindsey's passion for organizational development shows in her involvement in workshops, leadership programs and other group and individual training programs. Lindsey draws from her professional experience prior to joining Bluewater, as well as her degree from Central Michigan University in Interpersonal Communication and Public Communication, with a minor in Marketing.

Since joining the Bluewater team in the fall of 2014, Lindsey has led and participated in scores of client engagements. In addition to serving as Principal on dozens of Leadership programs, a few highlights include:

- Co-lead on Vision, Mission & Values retreat for a 50-year old professional services client
- Principal lead and trainer for a $1 billion professional services client
- Co-lead and project manager for Succession & Strategic Planning for a large family business client
- Principal lead and Job benchmarking expert, including over 20 job benchmarks for a single client
- Co-lead and content strategist on Bluewater's acclaimed *Leadership Rising* program
- Co-lead on a Strategic Planning retreat and full plan for a third-generation large family conglomerate
- Principal lead on *DreamSMALL*, Bluewater's impactful goal setting & attainment program

Lindsey is an avid Detroit Red Wings fan (with a special place for Steve Yzerman in her heart), and currently lives near Frederick, Maryland with her husband Gabe, and her daughter, Maggie, and son, Barrett.

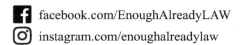

facebook.com/EnoughAlreadyLAW
instagram.com/enoughalreadylaw

Made in the USA
Middletown, DE
16 March 2021